Denali

Denali

A Journey of Friendship and Perseverance

Paul Schattenberg

SCHATTENBERG PUBLISHING

Schattenberg Publishing
Austin, Texas

First published in the United States of America, 2025

ISBN 979-8-9930464-0-2 (Hardback)
ISBN 979-8-9930464-1-9 (Paperback)
ISBN 979-8-9930464-2-6 (eBook)

Library of Congress Control Number: 2025924990

1st Printing

Printed in the United States of America

First Edition

Designed and edited by Paul Schattenberg

For my brother, Mark, whose strength, selflessness, and quiet wisdom guided us—on the mountain and in life. This journey, like so many others, was better because you were part of it.

"In every walk with nature one receives far more than he seeks."
– JOHN MUIR, STEEP TRAILS (1918)

Foreword

When I think about Denali, I do not just think about the summit or the storms. I think about my brother. Paul, this book exists because of you. Not because you stood on the glacier every step of the way, but because you chose the harder kind of courage, the kind that doesn't get photographs or summit records. When you turned back, you did not leave the climb. You became its lifeline. From the forests of Talkeetna, piecing together an antenna with Dad, you sent weather updates up the mountain that kept us moving forward. From a distance, you carried us.

Climbs are often measured in vertical feet and summit days. But I've come to believe the real measure is in the people who make the journey possible. You were that for me. You still are.

This book tells the story of our Denali expedition from a perspective only the author could provide. It captures the spirit of the climb, the weight of our decisions, and the bonds that carried us through. I'm grateful that our journey is being told, not just for what happened on the mountain, but for what it meant.

You've taught me that strength isn't always about pressing on. It is also about knowing when to hold back. Leadership isn't always about standing in front. It is often about standing behind, steady and unseen, until others need you most.

I offer this foreword with deep respect for the mountain and even deeper gratitude for you. Whatever Denali gave us, whether perspective, endurance, or healing, it gave through your presence, both near and far.

– Mark Schattenberg

Introduction

There are climbs that test your strength, and then there are climbs that test your soul. This is the story of one such climb, not just a push to the summit of Denali but a journey toward healing, brotherhood, and rediscovery.

When we began this expedition, the goal seemed straight-forward: summit the tallest peak in North America. But Denali quickly reminded us that no journey on her slopes is ever just physical. The real challenge was something deeper, something harder to quantify in feet or elevation gain.

For Mark, this climb was never about bragging rights or beating a record. It was about proving to himself that life after devastating injury still had room for meaning, for mountains, and for the quiet triumphs that come from pressing on when every part of you wants to stop. His story, more than any one summit photo, is what this book exists to share.

For Paul, the decision to descend early wasn't failure, it was wisdom. His continued role from below, working with their dad to build a homemade antenna in the forests of Talkeetna and feeding critical weather data up the mountain, became a lifeline in more ways than one. His withdrawal wasn't the end of his part in the climb; it was the beginning of a quieter kind of support, no less courageous.

And for Brandon, the steady companion and loyal friend, the mountain revealed not just the weight of his pack, but the deeper weight of being present for someone working their way back to themselves. His strength, silent, constant, and true, was an anchor during the storm.

This book is not only about reaching the summit. It's about friendship, vulnerability, and resilience. It's about frozen mornings and crevasse-marked paths. It's about wind that howls through the soul, and the radio voices that cut through the silence to say, "We're still with you."

Denali did not make it easy. She never does.

But in her unforgiving beauty, she gave us something far more enduring than a summit. She gave us perspective. Purpose. And the kind of bond that only comes from walking through suffering and wonder side by side.

May this story honor the mountain, the men who climbed her, and the quiet grace of those who support from the ground below.

CHAPTER ONE

The Call to Adventure

The mountains had always called to Mark, especially in the quiet moments when life felt most uncertain. But Denali was different. It wasn't just a mountain. For Mark, it was a reckoning, a chance to reclaim a sense of purpose that had slowly eroded since that morning run for coffee. One moment he'd been flowing down the familiar road, his body moving with the practiced grace of an elite endurance athlete. The next, screeching tires, impact, darkness. He still remembered swimming back to consciousness on the wrong side of the guardrail, the metallic taste of blood in his mouth, and the urgent voices of EMTs floating above him like distant echoes.

The hospital stay hadn't been easy, especially during COVID-19, with restrictions that kept him isolated from the support of family and friends. It was what came after that truly tested him, the grinding months of physical therapy, the way his once-finely tuned body now betrayed him at the simplest tasks. Each milestone in his recovery felt like a mockery of what he'd lost: his first steps without assistance, celebrated by nurses who didn't know he'd once run hundred-mile ultramarathons through mountain ranges; his first 'successful' jog around the block, when his body had once flowed through trails like water.

But it wasn't just the physical toll. Something deeper had fractured that morning, a fundamental trust in his own capabilities, a confidence built over thousands of miles and countless summits. His body had healed, at least according to the medical charts, but that internal compass that had always pointed him toward the next challenge, the next peak, the next impossible goal...that remained stubbornly broken. Until Denali called.

Denali wasn't just another climb. It was a reckoning with himself, a chance to reforge that broken compass in the unforgiving Alaskan ice. Every step up its slopes would be a step back toward the person he had been that morning before the world tilted on its axis. Or perhaps, toward someone new entirely.

For the past year, Mark had poured everything into planning this expedition. He had always been the planner, the one who obsessed over every detail, every ounce of gear, every route, and contingency plan. He had memorized the weather patterns, the terrain, the logistical hurdles. For Mark, every possible scenario had to be accounted for. This was Denali, after all. There was no margin for error.

Mark sat at the window of his Idaho home, the early morning sun casting long beams across the floor of his gear room. His pack leaned against the wall, zipped and ready, its seams taut with the weight of careful preparation. He traced a finger over the scars on his ankle, the ones that never fully faded.

On the wall above his desk hung a photo of him, Paul, and Brandon, taken on a summit years ago, their faces sunburned and beaming, arms slung over one another. He found himself staring at it more often lately. Outside, the mountains of Idaho shimmered faintly in the distance, beautiful but small compared to what lay ahead. He felt a fleeting tremor of doubt. He had faced steep climbs before, but none with stakes like this.

His phone buzzed, and Paul's name flashed across the screen. Mark swiped to answer the video call, trying to shake off the feeling as his brother's steady voice greeted him.

"You all set?" Paul asked, though his tone carried a trace of hesitation. They both knew Denali was different. One misstep here could mean more than just a bruised ego.

Mark angled his phone so Paul could see the gear lined up behind him. "Ready as I'll ever be. Everything's double-checked."

Paul smiled, but his brow furrowed. "Good, but remember, Denali can be...unpredictable. Weather up there is a whole different game."

"I know." Mark's response was quick, but he felt the weight behind Paul's words. They had both read the stories about climbers who underestimated Denali, who trusted their training over the mountain's whims. For them, the consequences had been final.

Paul seemed to read his brother's unease. "We'll have my radio tracking the weather and generating satellite imagery every step of the way," he said, his voice calm. "If anything's coming, we'll know before it hits."

"You don't know how much that helps," Mark admitted, the tension in his voice easing. Paul's technical know-how was a steady hand against Denali's volatile nature.

The conversation was interrupted by a familiar face joining the call. Brandon popped up on the screen, grinning as always.

"Am I late, or did you guys start early?" Brandon asked, leaning back in his chair with the easygoing confidence that had always been a part of his personality.

"Right on time," Mark said, his mood lifting at the sight of his best friend. Brandon had been a part of every major adventure Mark had undertaken, from long-distance kayaking marathons to grueling mountain climbs. They'd been through it all together, and Denali was just the latest in a long string of challenges they'd taken on.

"Got all your gear packed?" Paul asked, glancing over at the screen.

"Packed, and nothing forgotten," Brandon replied confidently. "I'm ready."

"Good," Mark said, nodding in satisfaction. He knew Brandon would have his gear in order. If there was one thing he could count on, it was that Brandon never forgot anything.

"Once we meet up tomorrow, we'll go over everything again before we head out."

The conversation turned to planning, with Mark leading the discussion. He laid out the exact timeline for when they'd arrive in Talkeetna, how they'd get their final gear checks done, and when they'd fly out to Denali Base Camp. Paul added his input on the weather patterns he'd been watching, and Brandon offered his usual encouragement, reminding them all to stay flexible in case plans had to change.

As the call wound down, Mark felt a growing sense of anticipation. Tomorrow, they would all be in Alaska. Tomorrow, they would be on the brink of something monumental.

"You guys ready for this?" Paul asked, his voice breaking through the quiet that had settled over the conversation. His tone was light, but the question carried the weight of the journey they were about to embark on.

Mark looked at his gear one last time, the culmination of a year's worth of planning and preparation. "Yeah," he said softly. "I'm ready."

"More than ready," Brandon chimed in, his grin still wide. "Let's do this."

Paul smiled, his face illuminated by the glow of his maps and radio equipment. "Then it's settled. Tomorrow, we meet in Talkeetna. After that, it's just us and the mountain."

Δ Δ Δ

The next day, Talkeetna hummed with energy. Climbers and adventurers filled the streets, their packs bulging with gear, their faces reflecting a mix of excitement and nerves. Mark stepped out of the small car that had brought him from the airport, and the sharp bite of the Alaskan air hit him, mingling with the scent of pine and woodsmoke clinging to the cool morning. Each breath felt like inhaling shards of ice, refreshing yet sharp. It was a jarring reminder that this wasn't home territory; it was Denali's domain.

Talkeetna had a rugged charm to it, with wooden buildings and dirt roads framed by the towering peaks in the distance. But for all its rustic appeal, it remained the gateway to Denali and the final stop for climbers before stepping onto the mountain. For Mark, it marked the threshold to the ascent that had loomed so large in his mind for the past year.

Mark's arrival in Talkeetna felt like the final confirmation that this was happening. Inside the main lodge, the room was filled with the clatter of gear and the murmur of voices, punctuated by the soft hum of a coffee machine behind the counter. The bitter aroma mingled with the sharp metallic tang of crampons and ice axes stacked along the walls, while the low light cast long shadows across the room. Surrounded by fellow climbers, he felt a flicker of shared anticipation, though beneath it all lay the same tension he'd seen in his own reflection. Each climber was there for something, whether thrill, victory, or redemption. This wasn't just another climb.

Mark dropped his pack by the door and scanned the room for familiar faces. It didn't take long to spot Paul, who was hunched over a table littered with maps and his ever-present radio, decoding fresh weather reports and satellite images.

Paul barely glanced up as Mark approached, too absorbed in his analysis.

"Good timing," Paul said, still focused on his task. "Winds are holding steady for now. It looks like we'll have a decent window, but you know Denali. That can change in an hour."

Mark smiled, his nerves calming a little in the presence of his brother's familiar intensity. "You'd know. Anything else to worry about?"

Paul finally looked up, his face thoughtful but not overly concerned. "Not right now, but I'll keep monitoring. Once we get up there, I'll be able to give us a clearer picture. I'll pull the latest weather data tomorrow morning before we fly out."

Mark nodded, grateful to have Paul's technical expertise on their side. Paul's ability to decode satellite images and predict weather patterns had saved them more than once on past trips, and Mark knew they'd need every edge they could get on this mountain.

Brandon arrived not long after, his grin as wide as ever. He stepped into the lodge with his usual relaxed air, effortlessly hoisting his pack onto the nearest table as though it weighed nothing.

"Man, you guys act like this is a life-or-death mission," Brandon joked, but there was a seriousness behind his eyes that belied the lightness of his tone. He knew the stakes as well as they did. "I thought we were here to enjoy the view."

Mark replied with a smirk, shaking his head. "I guess someone has to keep the mood light."

"That's what I'm here for," Brandon said, his grin never wavering. He had always been the one to break the tension, to remind them why they did these things in the first place. For Brandon, the adventure was as important as the outcome.

With everyone there, they headed out, the lodge falling behind them as they made their way toward Talkeetna Air Taxi. It wasn't a short walk. The airport was at least a mile from the town center. The air was crisp, the scent of pine needles filling their lungs as they walked along the dusty road.

As they approached, the iconic Talkeetna Air Taxi building came into view. It was a rustic log cabin with a wide porch adorned with colorful flower baskets. Its weathered wood blended seamlessly with the surrounding Alaskan wilderness, and a large signboard reading "Talkeetna Air Taxi: McKinley Flights; Glacier Landings" welcomed them.

Inside, the air buzzed with a quiet but palpable energy. A small group of climbers stood near a large map of Denali, their conversations low but animated. Being among the first climbers of the season, Mark, Paul, and Brandon found the space less crowded than they'd expected, though no less alive with anticipation.

A cheerful woman behind the counter greeted them with a warm smile. "Welcome to Talkeetna Air Taxi," she said, her voice steady and inviting. "I'm Emily, and I'll be guiding you through the process."

Emily wasted no time, diving into the essentials. She explained the weight restrictions for their gear, noting a limit of 125 pounds per person with $2 per pound for anything extra, and highlighted how weather conditions could affect their flight schedule. Mark, the meticulous planner, jotted down every word in his notebook, his face a mask of focus. Brandon leaned casually against the wall, taking it all in with an air of calm. Paul, ever analytical, asked pointed questions about timing and contingencies, his mind already mapping out possibilities.

The pilot, a young but seasoned professional, stepped forward next. His voice carried a mix of awe and caution as he shared stories from past flights to the glacier. He spoke of Denali's unpredictable nature, such as the shifting winds, sudden storms, and treacherous conditions that could turn routine landings into high-stakes maneuvers. "The flight to Base Camp will take about an hour," he concluded, "assuming the weather stays as clear as it is now."

As the pilot spoke, Mark felt his adrenaline surge. The mountain, once a distant dream, was now within reach.

Emily gestured toward a small safe behind the counter. "We have a secure safe here for wallets, passports, and keys since you won't need those on the mountain."

Mark glanced at Paul and Brandon, starting to reach into his pocket.

"You can do that the day you head out to the glacier," Emily added. "No need to hand them over just yet."

The act felt symbolic, even in anticipation, as it marked a final shedding of their everyday identities as they prepared to step into the unknown.

Emily continued, "Across the street at the pavilion, you can lay out your gear, get it weighed, and store any non-valuables in the containers."

Once they finished at the Talkeetna Air Taxi building, they made their way to the pavilion to complete their final checks.

The late morning sun gleamed on the polished metal of their ice axes and crampons. Mark worked meticulously, ensuring every item on his list was accounted for, while Paul double-checked the weight distribution of their packs. Brandon sorted through their food supplies, organizing meals into neat bundles for each stage of the climb and dividing them among the group.

"Utensils?" Mark asked.

Paul held up his set but seemed distracted as he inspected the rest of his gear. "Got it," he said, still preoccupied with the rest of his gear.

By the time they returned to the air taxi office, Emily had news. "You have two options," she said. "You can fly out early tomorrow morning to beat the storm, or you can wait until it clears in a few days."

Mark, Paul, and Brandon huddled together to discuss. Flying out early meant more time on the mountain but also carried risks if the storm approached faster than expected. Waiting would reduce the storm risk but delay their climb and limit their time on the mountain.

Mark broke the silence. "Let's go tomorrow. More days on the mountain means more time to acclimatize at altitude and have larger windows for the summit."

Paul nodded in agreement, and Brandon grinned. "We've got this!"

"Sounds good," Emily replied. "Just remember, you'll need to complete your National Park Service orientation and get your climbing permit tomorrow morning before the flight. It's mandatory for all climbers heading to Denali."

The trio nodded, knowing their schedule for the next day was tight. First, the orientation with the rangers, where they'd learn about safety protocols and crevasse dangers, along with how to use the Clean Mountain Cans, the required containers climbers use to pack out human waste, before heading straight to the air taxi to start their journey.

As the sun dipped below the horizon, painting the sky in hues of pink and orange, Mark, Paul, and Brandon ventured back into Talkeetna. The air carried a faint chill, the kind that hinted at the wilderness surrounding the small town. Main Street was alive with its rustic charm: wooden storefronts with carved signs, flower boxes brimming with hardy blooms, and locals chatting on benches as the last of the day's light softened the edges of the scene.

The trio wandered at an unhurried pace, taking in the atmosphere. Talkeetna felt timeless, as if it existed in its own rhythm, untouched by the fast pace of the modern world. It was easy to imagine the town's early days, when adventurers and gold seekers walked these very streets, their hearts set on the unknown.

Dinner at Latitude 62 was both hearty and comforting. The cozy, wood-paneled dining room buzzed with activity, a mix of climbers sharing plans for Denali and locals catching up over drinks. The smell of sizzling burgers and rich seafood filled the air, making the trio realize just how hungry they were after their long day of preparation.

They settled into a corner table, flipping through the menu while chatting about the upcoming climb. Mark, craving something hearty, ordered the Beer Battered Halibut, paired with a side of fries and coleslaw. Paul, ever practical, chose the Zesty Chicken Sandwich, marinated and topped with pepper jack cheese, opting for a lighter meal to keep his energy steady. Brandon, true to his adventurous spirit, went all-in with the Bacon Wrapped Jalapeños appetizer and the Mexi Burger, his plate piled high with fries and salsa.

The food arrived quickly, steaming and perfectly plated. Mark's crispy halibut was tender and flaky, the coleslaw adding a refreshing crunch to each bite. Paul's sandwich was juicy and packed with flavor, the pepper jack cheese giving it just the right kick. Brandon's jalapeños were smoky, spicy, and wrapped in crispy bacon. "A masterpiece!" He declared between bites. The Mexi Burger didn't disappoint either, with its melty cheese and jalapeño kick making every mouthful a burst of flavor.

As they ate, the room seemed to hum with shared excitement. At the bar, Brandon overheard a joke about an "Alaskan-sized appetite" and laughed along, his easy grin earning him nods from a group of locals. Paul leaned back in his chair, a rare look of calm crossing his face as he sipped his iced tea. Mark quietly took it all in, mentally checking off the day's accomplishments while savoring the moment of reprieve.

For dessert, they ordered a slice of Strawberry Rhubarb Pie to share, its sweet-tart filling a perfect end to the meal. As the last bites disappeared, they leaned back with satisfied sighs, their focus already shifting to the next day's challenges.

After their meal, they wandered past the historic Fairview Inn. Its wooden facade glowed under the golden lights strung along its porch. Mark paused, staring at the building's etched sign, its lettering worn from the passing years. The inn was a monument to the climbing community, its walls bearing witness to countless tales of triumph, heartbreak, and camaraderie. Mark imagined climbers sitting there in the days before their ascents, their anticipation and nerves likely mirroring his own. He couldn't help but feel the weight of history pressing softly against him.

Their walk ended at the banks of the Susitna River. The water flowed dark and steady under the twilight sky, the faint sound of its current blending with the whispers of the wind. Across the horizon, Denali stood like a sentinel, its silhouette stark and awe-inspiring. The snowy peaks reflected the fading light, glowing faintly as if they held their own quiet fire. Around it, smaller peaks seemed to bow in reverence, mere foothills compared to the giant. Denali's presence dominated the landscape, dwarfing everything around it.

They stood in silence, their thoughts unspoken but shared. For the past year, they had planned, trained, and dreamed of this climb. Now, standing beneath the shadow of the great mountain, the reality of the challenge began to take shape. It wasn't just the physical task ahead; it was the mental, emotional, and spiritual journey they were about to undertake.

Later, they returned to the lodge, nestled among the pines. The rustic cabin was simple but inviting, its wooden beams and small windows capturing the essence of Talkeetna's rugged charm. Mark stretched out in his bunk, staring at the wooden ceiling above him. The soft breathing of Paul and Brandon filled the room, grounding him in the moment. A distant howl echoed through the night, a wolf's cry that sent a shiver down his spine, not of fear, but of awe.

Tomorrow, they would leave this comfort behind. They would trade warm beds and soft light for the raw, unforgiving beauty of the glacier. But for now, in the stillness of the Alaskan night, Mark let his thoughts settle.

△ △ △

The next morning, Mark, Paul, and Brandon arrived early at the Walter Harper Talkeetna Ranger Station. The sun had just begun to rise, casting a soft golden glow over the quiet streets of Talkeetna. Outside the station stood a whiteboard, its surface marked with neat columns of numbers.

2022 Climbing Season	Denali	Foraker
Registered Climbers	1028	17
On Mountain	33	2
Off Mountain	0	0
Summits	0	0
Backcountry Users: 73		

Mark paused in front of the board; his breath visible in the morning chill. "We're just a number," he murmured, his voice tinged with awe.

Brandon nodded. "But think about it. Every number up there is someone chasing the same dream."

Paul added, "It's a good reminder of how much planning and effort goes into keeping track of everyone on the mountain."

The trio stood in silence for a moment before stepping inside.

The warm air inside the ranger station was a welcome contrast to the crisp morning outside. A small crowd of climbers milled about. The room was filled with a quiet hum of anticipation, and the walls were lined with posters of Denali and its surrounding peaks.

At the front desk stood Katie, her name tag gleaming under the fluorescent lights. She greeted each group with a warm but efficient demeanor, ensuring the morning progressed smoothly. When it was their turn, she glanced at her clipboard.

"Good morning," she said. "Here for the Denali orientation?"

"That's right," Mark replied. "We're Team Moustache Madness."

Katie chuckled softly. "Interesting name. Looks like you're all set." She glanced toward the door. "We're still waiting on a few more climbers, but once they're here, we'll get started. Feel free to look around and grab a seat in the meantime."

While waiting for the ranger presentation to begin, Paul's attention wandered to a polished wooden plaque mounted on the wall near the front desk. The engraved letters read "Mislow-Swanson Denali Pro Award," and beneath them was a brief summary.

The plaque explained the program, which began in 1998 as a partnership between the National Park Service and climbing equipment manufacturer Pigeon Mountain Industries. The award honored climbers who exhibited the highest standards in safety, self-sufficiency, Leave No Trace ethics, and helping fellow mountaineers. Each season, mountaineering rangers recognized climbers for exceptional expedition behavior, awarding them a Denali Pro lapel pin.

Paul leaned in closer, reading the note about John Mislow and Andrew Swanson, whose names now graced the award. The two men had won for their exemplary climbing ethics in 2000 but tragically died in a climbing fall on the West Rib in 2009. Their families had worked with the park to ensure the program continued in their memory, an enduring legacy of respect for the mountain and its climbers.

Brandon, noticing Paul's interest, walked over. "Pretty incredible, huh?" he said, his voice low.

Paul nodded. "It's a reminder of what this is all about: responsibility, awareness, and looking out for each other. Denali demands nothing less."

The two stood in silence for a moment before the ranger called for everyone's attention, signaling the start of the orientation.

The trio settled into the presentation room, where a few other climbers were already seated. Once the last group arrived, Katie began the orientation, standing in front of a large map of Denali.

"So, here's what we're going to cover today," she began, her tone shifting to one of authority. "Safety procedures, crevasse risks, proper waste management, and radio protocols. But first, let me say this: Denali is unlike any mountain you've climbed. Respect her, and she'll reward you with an experience of a lifetime. Disrespect her, and she won't hesitate to remind you who's in charge."

Mark nodded, taking mental notes, while Paul leaned forward, his attention sharp. Brandon, as always, had a calm expression but listened intently.

Katie moved seamlessly through her presentation, pointing out key landmarks on the map and explaining the importance of wands for marking gear caches in the snow. She demonstrated the proper way to secure a Clean Mountain Can and emphasized the critical need to avoid leaving anything behind on the mountain.

"Any questions?" Katie asked as she wrapped up the session.

Mark raised his hand. "If we need to call for help, how quickly can a ranger team respond?"

Katie's face grew serious. "That depends on your location and the weather. Rescue operations aren't instantaneous, especially at higher altitudes. And just so we're clear, if you require rescue, your climb ends there. No exceptions."

Paul nodded in understanding. "Got it. Better to avoid needing one altogether."

"Exactly," Katie replied. "Now, let's get you your permits and make sure everything's in order."

At the back of the room, they waited their turn as Katie processed the climbers ahead of them. When their turn came, Katie handed Brandon a letter-sized sheet of paper bearing their names and team name, stamped with the official seal of Denali National Park.

"This is your permit," Katie said. "It confirms your authorization to climb and identifies your team to rangers on the mountain. Keep it safe."

Brandon carefully folded the paper and tucked it into his jacket pocket.

As they stepped outside, Brandon grinned. "We're officially climbing Denali."

Mark smirked. "No turning back now."

"Not that we ever planned to," Paul added with a dry chuckle.

They made their way back to Talkeetna Air Taxi, where Emily greeted them at the counter. "Welcome back! Did you all get your permit?" she said, glancing up from her clipboard.

Brandon reached into his jacket and produced the letter-sized sheet of paper, handing it to Emily.

"Sure did!" Brandon said.

She scanned it quickly, jotted down a few notes, and gave a satisfied nod. "All set. Now, wallets, passports, and valuables."

One by one, they handed over their items, the act feeling oddly final, which Emily placed into individual plastic bags labeled with their names before locking them in the secure safe behind her.

Outside, they retrieved their gear from the pavilion. The air taxi crew worked quickly, weighing each pack and loading it onto the airplane.

The pilot, who had flown this route more times than he could count, gave them a nod before gesturing toward the plane. Mark climbed into the cabin, settling into his seat as the engine's vibrations rumbled through the floor. His stomach swirled with a blend of anxiety and excitement.

As the plane taxied down the runway, Mark looked out the window. The snowy peaks of Denali glimmered in the distance, their sharp edges softened by the morning light.

The plane took off with a lurch, climbing steadily into the sky. The hum of the engine thrummed through his bones, a steady vibration that felt like the pulse of something alive beneath him. Outside the window, the Alaskan wilderness spread out in all directions. Rivers wound through dense forests like silver veins, and jagged, snow-capped peaks rose into a sky washed pale by the early morning light.

The chill inside the plane felt sharper, almost biting, and Mark instinctively pulled his jacket closer around him. Beside him, Brandon and Paul were silent, each lost in their thoughts, their faces cast in the pale glow from the window. The closer they got to Denali, the more Mark felt the weight settle in his chest. Every mile brought him closer to the mountain and to whatever parts of himself he was about to confront. He wasn't just looking at the mountain; he was looking at a force that seemed to breathe and shift, daring him to try.

The plane dipped slightly as they neared the glacier, and his stomach lurched with a mix of nerves and exhilaration. The harsh brightness of the snow-filled landscape below reflected back up at them, filling the cabin with an almost blinding light.

"This is it," Brandon whispered, his voice filled with a quiet awe as he leaned closer to the window.

Mark nodded, his heart pounding in his chest. The mountain was breathtaking in its immensity, but there was something almost ominous about it, like it was daring them to try.

As the plane descended toward Base Camp, the glacier came into view, a vast, frozen desert stretching out beneath them. The plane touched down with a soft rumble, kicking up a cloud of snow as they landed. The cold hit immediately, sharp and biting, cutting through their layers like a knife. But none of them flinched.

All three looked up at the towering peak of Denali, their breath hanging in the air as they took in the magnitude of the moment. For Mark, there was no turning back. Each step ahead would be a step away from his broken past, or a final reckoning with it on the mountain's icy slopes.

CHAPTER TWO

Landing at Base Camp

The hum of the plane's engine faded into the crisp, thin air as it lifted off the glacier, leaving Mark, Paul, and Brandon standing in the vast white wilderness of Denali. The moment they inhaled, all three of them coughed at once. The air was so cold and dry it hit their lungs like a warning. It wasn't the thinness of the atmosphere but the bite of it, the way the glaciated air seemed to pull every drop of moisture from their mouths as they drew it in.

Their lungs adjusted after a moment, but the message was clear: on Denali, even breathing was work.

The glacier stretched out endlessly beneath their feet, a frozen expanse of snow and ice that glistened under the afternoon sun. Denali's peaks loomed stark and towering in the distance, while the sprawling, frozen desert of Base Camp stretched out before them.

As the plane disappeared into the clouds, Mark shifted, feeling the snow crunch beneath his boots as he took a tentative step forward. The step felt like a quiet defiance, a small victory over the life he'd been fighting to rebuild. Out here, every footfall meant progress toward the summit and toward himself. The cold bit through his layers, and he could almost feel the weight of the mountain settling over them. They were finally here. It wasn't just the altitude that struck him; it was the quiet, heavy presence of Denali, as if the mountain itself watched them, daring them to come closer.

"This is it," Mark said with a grin, his breath turning to mist in the freezing air.

All three of them looked up at the towering peaks. The wind tugged at their jackets, carrying with it the bite of Denali's icy breath. For a brief moment, there was silence between them, each taking in the enormity of the task ahead.

Before they could start the ascent, there was work to be done at Base Camp. The first moments after arrival always felt surreal, transitioning from the organized chaos of the town to the vast, quiet expanse of the mountain. Every step had a purpose, and everything they did had consequences. Base Camp was their last link to any semblance of normality, but even here, the wild isolation of Denali was undeniable.

Gabbi, the Base Camp leader, approached them as they organized their gear on the snow near the landing strip. She was a friendly, experienced guide with years spent managing Base Camp and helping climbers get started on Denali. Her presence was calming, a steady voice of authority in a landscape where the rules could change at any moment.

"You three just off the plane?" Gabbi called out, waving as she trudged across the snow toward them.

"Fresh from Talkeetna," Mark said, slinging his pack onto the snow.

"I'm Gabbi. I run Base Camp." She gave them a quick once-over, clearly sizing them up. "You don't look green, so I'll keep this short."

She gestured over her shoulder with her thumb. "Toilet's that way. Cache zones ahead. You're digging for your cache, not dumping. Got it?"

Brandon chuckled. "Wouldn't dream of it."

Gabbi cracked a half-smile, then glanced toward the northwest horizon, where a faint wall of gray hung over the distant ridges. "Clouds usually ride in from that way, late afternoon or overnight. You've got time, but don't waste it."

She turned back to them and added, "Just so you know, park rangers broadcast a weather report every evening over the open radio channel. That'll cover the high camps at and above 14,000-Foot Camp and the summit. Make sure your radios are tuned and on by then if you're climbing past Camp 2."

She paused, letting that settle, then said dryly, "Denali doesn't care how strong you are. Just how prepared. I've seen marathoners bail and rookies summit. The mountain chooses."

She led them a short way farther. "Here's where you'll cache your food," she said, pointing toward the marked zone. "Make sure you dig deep enough. Snow melts fast up here, or it can pile on meters overnight. You don't want to come back to find

23

your wands completely buried or, worse, your cache melted out."

Gabbi glanced over at Mark, clearly the leader of the trio, and gestured toward the line of wands marking other caches in the snow. "Mark the perimeter with wands high enough so you can find it later and pile more snow on top when you're done to guard against melt."

Mark nodded, his mind already ticking off each detail. This was just another step in the plan, one more thing to account for. "Got it," he said, turning to Paul and Brandon. "Let's get the cache dug, and then we'll head for Camp 1."

Paul adjusted his pack and nodded, though he didn't say much. Brandon was already pulling a shovel from his pack before anyone said a word, his breath turning to mist in the cold as he stepped into the snow.

Gabbi continued, her voice steady. "No need to set up a tent here if you're heading to Camp 1 today. Just make sure your cache is secure. Camp 1 is about five miles out. The weather's fine for now. You'll want to be on your way before it shifts."

"Thanks for the heads-up," Paul said, glancing at the sky. Unlike earlier climbs, Paul wasn't constantly pulling out his radio for updates. He had scheduled transmission times in his list, knowing exactly when to expect weather updates. Paul would stick to his routine, checking in at each camp. On Denali, missing a single update could mean walking straight into a storm. His focus now was on getting to Camp 1 before anything changed.

Gabbi gave them a final nod. "Stay safe out there!"

With the orientation done, Mark, Paul, and Brandon set to work on the cache. The snow beneath their boots crunched with every step, and the wind whipped lightly across the glacier, the chill a constant reminder of where they were. Mark, as always, took charge, driving his shovel into the packed snow with a satisfying thud, then checking the depth and stability as they worked. Every detail mattered up here, and Mark wouldn't leave anything to chance.

"Let's make sure this is deep enough," Mark said, his voice steady as he worked. "We can't risk losing our backup food if things go sideways."

Paul paused, leaning on his shovel. "It's starting to feel like we are digging our own escape route."

"Remind me again who we're caching this for?" Brandon asked, flicking a chunk of snow aside. "Future-us or rescue-us?"

Mark looked up. "Both."

The cache, to Mark, was like a mental insurance policy. They all knew the risks of a climb like this. Plans could change at a moment's notice. Storms could roll in, accidents could happen. Having supplies stashed away could mean the difference between survival and catastrophe. It was a safety net, but Mark treated it with the same seriousness he approached the rest of the climb. Every detail mattered.

Brandon, ever the optimist, worked with a lightness to his movements, tossing snow aside with ease. "When we're on our way down, all we'll need to do is dig it up and get out of here."

Paul, quieter than usual, methodically shoveled snow alongside them. His eyes flicked now and again to the horizon.

While Paul tracked the technicalities like weather and equipment, the reality was that all three of them were seasoned climbers. Mark, Paul, and Brandon each brought years of experience to this climb. Collectively, they were the mind of the team, contributing equally to the strategy and decision-making.

As they dug deeper, Paul spoke up, his voice low but thoughtful. "I'll check the radio at Camp 1. We're still in the clear, but I want to know when the next transmission comes in."

Mark nodded, appreciating his brother's caution. "Let's focus on getting there first."

They worked efficiently, digging until the pit was wide and deep enough to meet the National Park Service requirements. Brandon marked the perimeter with bright orange wands, sticking them into the snow around the cache.

Paul leaned on his shovel and glanced down into the hole. "You think it's deep enough?"

Brandon chuckled, "Deep enough to throw a snowmobile into!"

Their cache bag was already packed with extra food and emergency supplies spread across several plastic bags inside. Each bag was organized to guard against snowmelt; if one bag failed, the others would stay dry. Redundancy in everything was the rule.

Paul and Brandon handed the bundle down into the hole to Mark. Mark knelt and adjusted it, settling the load evenly into the base before standing and climbing out.

Then they shoveled snow over the top, packing it tight to insulate and conceal it. Paul added a few extra markings alongside Brandon's bright orange wands just in case fresh snow buried everything.

It wasn't glamorous work, but it was essential.

Once the cache was complete, Mark stepped back, satisfied. "Good. That's done. Let's get moving before the light shifts."

They adjusted their packs and gear, clipping into the rope line as they prepared to leave Base Camp behind and make the five-mile trek to Camp 1. Mark led the way, feeling the familiar surge of energy he always experienced when transitioning from preparation to action.

Paul took his place in the middle. His pack weighed more than the others with the extra radio equipment, but he never complained. All three of them understood the role each played on the climb. Paul's strength was his eye for detail; he caught the threats they could not always see. Brandon, in the back, maintained his easy pace, his constant optimism like a steady pulse keeping the team moving forward.

They moved in silence for the first stretch, the only sounds being the soft crunch of snow under their snowshoes and the gentle flapping of their jackets in the wind.

For Mark, the silence wasn't just physical. It was the echo of something deeper, something broken. The rhythm of the mountain was familiar. The pulse of step, breath, and pole no longer felt effortless. It was as if he were still relearning trust in his own body, in the decisions that had once come instinctively.

Denali didn't care that he'd nearly lost it all. It didn't recognize past glory or injury. It asked only one thing: Are you ready?

The glacier was vast and empty, a seemingly endless sheet of ice with no shelter, no landmarks, only the raw, untouched wilderness. Each step seemed to stretch the world out farther; as they moved across the glacier, a silent reminder hung in the air. Denali had no loyalties. It did not matter how long they had trained or how carefully they had prepared. Here, only the mountain dictated the terms.

As they ascended toward Camp 1, the enormity of the glacier beneath them became more pronounced. Deep crevasses yawned open in the snow, dark, forbidding voids that seemed to swallow the light. Mark led them carefully, guiding them through the maze of hidden dangers. Each step had to be precise. There was no room for mistakes on this terrain.

As they moved, Mark found his thoughts drifting, the silence of the glacier giving way to the steady rhythm of his breathing. His muscles burned with each step, but it was a good kind of pain. It was the kind that reminded him he was alive, pushing himself beyond his limits. Denali was unlike any other mountain he had climbed. It was not just the altitude or the cold. It was the isolation. The feeling that, out here, nothing was guaranteed.

Brandon's voice cut through the quiet, light but purposeful. "You ever think about what it's going to feel like when we're at the top?"

Mark glanced back at him, the corners of his mouth lifting in a brief smile. "Not yet. We've still got a long way to go."

Brandon grinned, unfazed. "I'm already imagining it. Just us and the view."

They continued on, the climb to Camp 1 grueling but steady. By the time they reached their destination five hours later, the afternoon had begun to settle into a cold, muted blue, the light fading as shadows stretched across the snow. The wind had picked up slightly, adding a bite to the already frigid air.

With every step, Mark felt a weight lift, not just the physical load, but something deeper. Standing here, looking up at the towering summit, he felt closer to reclaiming the control he had lost that day on the road, one step at a time.

"We're here," he said, a hint of relief in his voice. He could feel the weight of the day's effort in his legs, but it was a good kind of exhaustion, the kind that told him they were moving in the right direction.

Paul stopped and surveyed the area, his eyes flicking across the glacier. It was wide open, exposed, but safe enough for the night. "Let's get camp set up before the wind gets worse."

Brandon did not hesitate. "I've got the tent poles!"

They worked quickly, setting up their tent and cook tent on the glacier and securing everything tightly down. The air had grown noticeably colder, the sky dimming as the day gave way to the long arctic twilight. They moved with purpose, every task efficient, every movement necessary. Here, efficiency was everything.

Mark stepped back, surveying their set-up, satisfied with how quickly they had set up camp. But as he took in the expanses of snow stretching up toward Denali's shadowed peak, a quiet realization settled over him. This was only the beginning. The challenges lay somewhere ahead, hidden in Denali's silent vastness and unpredictable moods. Mark felt a flicker of anticipation, and a touch of caution, at the thought. They had reached Camp 1, but Denali had yet to reveal its true face.

Inside the cook tent, the stove's warmth spread quickly, offering a brief barrier against the biting cold. The gentle hiss of boiling water felt oddly comforting, like the warmth of a distant memory they carried with them on this icy terrain. In this small circle of heat and camaraderie, it felt, if only for a moment, like they had carved out a refuge from the mountain's relentless hold. Mark crouched down, pulling out one of their freeze-dried meals and adding hot water to it. The smell of rehydrating beef stew filled the small space.

Paul rummaged through his pack, frowning. "I could've sworn I packed my utensils."

Brandon grinned, stirring his own meal. "Check again."

Paul dug deeper into his pack, frustration growing. "I know I brought them."

After another moment of searching, Paul gave up, shaking his head. "They may be buried deep in my backpack. May I borrow one of yours for now, Brandon?"

Brandon handed Paul his spare utensil without hesitation. "Here. Enjoy your stew with a knife."

Mark chuckled. "You're never going to live this down, Paul!"

They ate their meal in relative silence, the fatigue of the day settling into their bones. The warmth of the cook tent and the shared food provided a brief respite from the unforgiving cold outside.

Paul dug out his radio and synchronized it to his phone. The forecast hadn't shifted much. It was still calm through the next day, with a wind front building behind. He said nothing to the others, but he knew they should expect similar weather, gradually worsening by day's end.

They lingered a moment longer inside the cook tent after the meals were done, the hiss of the stove winding down. Mark looked at his friends, their flushed cheeks, the tight lines around their eyes, and felt something shift inside him.

Outside, Denali waited. But here, at this moment, they were warm, full, and together. It wasn't safety, but it was close.

"Tomorrow gets steeper," Paul said, standing up and stretching.

Brandon grinned. "Then we'd better rise to match it."

Mark smiled, pushing open the tent flap and stepping into the wind. The cold rushed over him like a wave, but for the first time in a long time, he didn't flinch.

CHAPTER THREE

The Path to Camp 2

S omething cold landed on Paul's face. He blinked up at the tent ceiling, just in time to catch another flake of frozen vapor drifting down like snow inside a snow globe. Their breath had condensed overnight and with every movement they made it rained back down on them as a silent reminder that comfort did not belong here, even in a tent.

"Frozen fog's coming for us," he muttered.

From the other side of the tent, Brandon groaned, still buried in his sleeping bag. "It's attacking."

Paul shifted with a low grunt; muscles stiff from the climb and the unrelenting cold that even made rest a minor act of endurance. He reached for the small weather radio by his side, fingers moving on instinct. First thing every morning, check the forecast.

He powered it on and synchronized it to his phone. Lines flickered on the screen, weather faxes decoding into the grayscale curves Paul had learned to trust. Paul leaned in closely, studying the incoming patterns with quiet focus.

Mark stirred next to him, tugging his sleeping bag tighter. The cold hung in the tent like fog, clinging to their gear, turning every breath visible. "Anything new?" he mumbled.

Paul shook his head. "Same as yesterday. Calm now, but wind is on its way."

"Awesome," Brandon said flatly. "I was hoping for a gentle, relaxing spa day."

Mark reached for the tent zipper. "Brace yourselves!"

Mark tugged the flap down, and a rush of glacial air sliced through the tent like a blade: metallic, dry, and biting. All three hissed involuntarily, the cold shocking them fully awake.

Outside, the world hadn't changed. The sun, locked in its perpetual high arc, cast everything in a pale, sterile glow. Shadows barely moved. It was strange to be in a place with no dawn or dusk, only soft light that never shifted.

They emerged from the tent one by one, wrapped in layers, their faces hidden behind fleece, goggles, and hoods. Only their breath gave them away, steam curling up in soft clouds. The glacier around them was still untouched. No footprints. No voices. Just three men in a field of silence.

They were among the first on the mountain this season, and the fresh, unmarked snow was a reminder that no clear path had yet been established.

Breaking down camp had to be efficient in the freezing conditions. First, they dismantled the main tent, carefully packing it away, followed by their other gear. Their hands worked quickly, the cold seeping through even the thickest layers of gloves. The howling wind was a constant reminder of the mountain's unpredictability.

Mark stood up, looking out across the vast expanse. "Let's get moving. We've got a long push today, and it's only going to get worse."

Brandon tightened his pack straps, shaking off the remnants of sleep. "I'm ready. Let's get it done before the weather turns on us."

Paul pulled out his GPS, loading the preloaded tracks from previous climbs. With no climbers ahead of them, the path was not as clear as it would be later in the season. They had to rely entirely on the GPS tracks from past climbers, making sure they stayed as close to the established routes as possible.

Mark took his place at the front of the rope line, leading them across the snowfield. Paul, in the middle, kept his eyes on the GPS, making sure they stayed on course, while Brandon brought up the rear. The vastness of the glacier stretched out in front of them, an endless, white expanse with no landmarks to guide them except for the tracks loaded into their devices.

They moved at a slow, steady pace, the snowshoes sinking into the fresh snow with every step. The wind bit at their faces, stinging their exposed skin as they trudged forward. The glacier felt eerily silent, with no other teams around and only the sound of their snowshoes crunching into the snow breaking the stillness.

After a few hours of trekking in near silence, Mark signaled for a break. They had been moving at a careful pace, knowing that rushing up Denali wasn't an option. Slow and steady was the key to surviving this mountain.

They dropped their packs.

For a moment, none of them spoke.

The landscape stretched out endlessly, white, and untouched, almost alien. A place that looked like it had never known a human footprint.

The peaks of Denali, towering high in the distance, looked deceptively close, but they knew better.

Denali played tricks.

Distances looked shorter than they were, and every summit seemed closer than reality allowed. It lured you in with the illusion of progress, then punished your belief in it.

Paul glanced ahead, squinting through wind-blown snow. "Still looks close."

"It always does," Mark said. "That's the Denali factor."

As they stood in silence, they heard the unmistakable sound of avalanches rumbling in the distance. They seemed to echo from all directions, going off like clockwork every five to ten minutes, far enough away that they could not pinpoint where they were coming from. It was an unsettling reminder of the mountain's power, a constant background noise that never let them forget the dangers that lay ahead.

"Those avalanches...they just keep going," Brandon said quietly, his voice barely cutting through the wind.

The rumble seemed to echo in his bones, a stark reminder of just how small they were out here. It was humbling, as though the mountain were warning them of what lay ahead.

They all sipped from their thermoses of coffee, the warmth a small comfort against the biting wind. The stillness around them felt almost suffocating, as if they were the only people left in this vast, frozen wilderness.

After a few more moments of rest, Mark checked his watch and motioned for them to move. "All right, break's over. Let's keep moving before the weather turns on us."

The wind began to pick up not long after they resumed their trek, howling across the glacier and kicking up snow that stung their faces. The calm, peaceful air they had experienced during their break had quickly shifted, and now visibility was starting to drop. The snow blew in swirls around them, making it harder to see the landscape ahead.

The wind clawed at them, finding every small gap in their layers, and biting into their exposed cheeks. Each gust felt sharper, colder, as if the mountain were testing their resolve.

Paul kept a close eye on his GPS, constantly checking their position as the visibility worsened. Visibility dropped to just a few feet ahead, the swirling snow blurring everything into a uniform white that made every direction look the same. But Paul's GPS kept them on track.

"Visibility's dropping fast," Paul called out over the wind. "We're still following the route, but it's going to get tough if this keeps up."

Mark squinted through the wind, feeling the cold biting at his exposed cheeks. "Let's keep close. We can push a little further."

But as the wind intensified and the visibility dropped to near zero, it became clear that they were not going to make it to Camp 2. The markers and landmarks they had expected to see were obscured by the whiteout conditions, and the risk of continuing without a clear view of the path was too great.

Mark scanned the swirling snow, squinting against the stinging cold. The decision weighed on him. They had planned to push through to Camp 2, but one wrong step could mean disaster in these conditions.

Mark stopped and turned to the others, who were barely visible through the swirling snow. "This is madness. We're not going to find Camp 2 like this." Mark said, his voice muffled.

"But we're close," Paul said, stepping beside him.

Mark shook his head. "Close doesn't matter if we fall into something we can't see."

Brandon gave a short nod. "Then we camp. Live to climb another day."

They all knew he was right. Pushing forward in such conditions would be reckless, and the risk of walking into a crevasse or unstable snow was too high. They immediately began searching for a suitable spot to set up camp.

The snowstorm made it hard to find a flat, stable surface, but after a while, they came across a small plateau. All three of them pulled out their avalanche probes, testing the ground beneath them to ensure it was safe. Each of them probed, working in silence as the sound of their probes sinking into the snow was drowned out by the wind.

After several minutes, they mutually agreed the ground was stable. "It's good," Mark said. "We can set up here."

They set to work, using their shovels to clear out a flat area for their tent. The wind was relentless, but they moved quickly, working together to create a safe space for camp. With each shovelful of snow, they built the windbreaker, packing it tightly around the perimeter of their camp to shield them from the worst of the wind.

Setting up the tent was war against wind and fatigue.

Paul's shoulders ached with every shovel strike. Mark's hands went numb twice, and he had to stomp them against his thighs. Brandon swore under his breath, ice clinging to his lashes.

No one talked. No one had to. They just worked, three figures against the storm. They left their packs outside, bringing only their sleeping bags and the day-kits into the tent.

The wind clawed at the tent walls, a relentless reminder that Denali did not offer comfort; however, the relative calm inside the tent was a welcome relief. They decided not to set up the cook tent due to the fierce wind. Safety came first, and they knew that. They huddled in their tent, wind howling just inches away.

Outside, the storm raged. Inside, the silence did not feel like safety, just a brief pause before the next test.

CHAPTER FOUR

The Long Night on the Plateau

They were pinned down in their tent, waiting out the storm, while the relentless wind outside rattled the fabric and pressed against the walls like an invisible weight. Inside, the cold gnawed at them despite the layers of clothing and sleeping bags they had wrapped around themselves. It wasn't enough to stop the chill from creeping in, sinking into their bones. The windbreaker they had built did its job, but the plateau felt exposed, vulnerable to the whims of Denali's fury.

Mark lay on his back, staring up at the darkened tent ceiling. The roar of the wind had become a constant companion, filling the silence and amplifying the sense of isolation. He could hear the others shifting in their sleeping bags, trying to get comfortable, but there was no comfort to be found. The cold was everywhere. It seemed impossible to escape it.

His mind wandered back to the years of preparation that had brought them here. Endless gear checks, route planning, and physical training, all carefully done for the climb. Mark had trained with the same intensity when he prepared for competitions in kayaking. He knew how to plan and persevere. But now, lying there in the dark, he realized that no amount of preparation could have readied them for the sheer unpredictability of Denali. The mountain had its own rules, and they were just temporary guests.

Brandon shifted beside him; his breath heavy in the freezing air. "I don't think I've ever felt this exposed on a mountain," he muttered.

Mark turned his head slightly, his voice low. "Yeah. Feels like the wind could rip us out of here any second."

Paul, who had been lying quietly for what felt like hours, finally spoke. His voice was hoarse, barely audible over the wind. "It's like the mountain's testing us."

Mark didn't respond right away. The mountain was always testing them, but this, this was different. Denali was vast, untamed. It wasn't just about surviving the climb; it was about surviving the mountain itself. Every gust of wind and every avalanche rumbling in the distance was a reminder that they were visitors in a place where nature held all the power.

Hours dragged by, the wind refusing to let up. Every gust felt like an invisible hand pressing against the walls of the tent, threatening to collapse it at any moment. The three men were silent for a while, each lost in his own thoughts, until Mark, feeling the tension build in the small space, decided to break the silence.

"One time, I was racing in the World Championships in Portugal," Mark said suddenly, his voice breaking through the wind like a flare in the dark.

Paul and Brandon both shifted slightly in their sleeping bags, not surprised. They had heard bits and pieces of this story before, but not the full thing. And now, hunkered down in the cold, it seemed like a good distraction. Mark didn't often talk about kayaking unless something inside him needed release.

"It was 2018. Marathon kayak. Roughly 30 kilometers of racing and over two hours on the water. I trained for years."

Paul said nothing, but Brandon offered a low whistle. "That the one with the portages?"

Mark nodded. "Yep. You're paddling hard, then you hit the shoreline, jump out, grab the kayak, and sprint down the course before getting back in. Over and over. Legs screaming, arms jelly, heart pounding. But you can't let up."

He paused a beat.

"There was this moment, two-thirds in, where I completely cracked. Body was done. But I looked over and saw this Hungarian racer pulling ahead. And something in me just...snapped into focus. I found another gear I didn't know existed."

Paul gave a small smile in the dark. "You've always had that gear."

"Not always," Mark said, quietly. "But that day, yeah. I crossed the line completely emptied. But I'd raced clean. No regrets. And that moment...it taught me something."

Brandon's voice was soft. "That you were stronger than you thought?"

Mark shook his head, the fabric of his sleeping bag rustling. "That sometimes it's not about strength. It's about clarity. About knowing why you're hurting and choosing it anyway."

For a moment, the tent was quiet again except for the wind. Then Brandon said, "Horseshoe Canyon."

Mark chuckled. "Oh, man...That crack climb!"

"Looked easy from the ground," Brandon said. "I remember thinking, 'This will be a warm-up.'"

Paul actually laughed. "Didn't you end up upside down at one point?"

"Yup. Halfway through, I was wedged in like a cork in a bottle. Couldn't move up, couldn't slide down. Just dangling there, totally humbled."

Mark nodded, grinning now. "I remember that roof section near the top. My pack kept swinging into the rock, throwing off my balance. Every hold felt like a gamble."

Brandon leaned his head back. "We topped out and collapsed in the dirt, totally thrashed. And I remember thinking, 'That was the best climb we've ever done.'"

Mark smiled. "Because we suffered well."

"Because we climbed well," Brandon corrected. "We didn't panic. We trusted each other. Every piece of gear, every placement. We earned that summit!"

Paul murmured, "That's what I miss sometimes. It's not about the summits or checkmarks but earning it. Knowing that every step and every choice mattered."

The tent quieted again, not with the emptiness of fatigue but with a fullness grounded in shared understanding.

Mark broke it gently. "I think that's why we're here. To find that again."

Brandon nodded slowly. "Yeah. This climb...it's our clean line. No shortcuts, no noise. Just us and the mountain, doing it the way it should be done."

The laughter and camaraderie lifted their spirits for a while. On Denali, every bit of encouragement mattered. Nature always had the upper hand, and they all knew it. Still, they were determined to press on.

Paul decided to check his radio, adjusting the frequency, trying to pick up anything that might cut through the static. The crackle of the radio filled the tent, and for a brief moment, distant voices came through. They were faint, hard to make out.

"They're out there," Paul said, leaning closer to the radio. "But we're surrounded by mountains. It's cutting us off."

He put the radio aside with a sigh. "We'll try again later."

Paul wasn't just listening for voices, though. His radio was set up to receive satellite imagery, a tool he relied on to get a better sense of the weather fronts moving across Alaska. He began adjusting the radio again and this time recording the satellite signals, knowing it would take over ten minutes for each image to come through. As the first satellite image started to form on his screen, he studied it, recognizing the cloud patterns and storm fronts over the region. The storm patterns over the region were thick, layered, and unyielding.

He sighed. "It's digging in. This storm's not going anywhere anytime soon," Paul said, studying the image with an edge of frustration. "We're hunkered down for a while."

Mark frowned but nodded. They had known this was a possibility. Storms could pin climbers down for days on Denali. Still, the reality of being stuck in a tent for an extended period was difficult to accept. They were here to climb, not sit around waiting for the weather to improve.

To pass the time, Mark pulled out his phone. Every movie had been downloaded well before the trip. There was no signal this far up Denali. Thanks to his solar panel and power bank, the battery was still holding strong. He set up the phone in the middle of the tent, and they huddled closer, watching one of the movies he'd brought along for moments like this. It wasn't much, but it kept their minds off the relentless wind outside, offering a small escape.

After the movie ended, the wind had picked up even more, its howl a near constant now. They knew they weren't going anywhere tonight, maybe not even tomorrow, if the storm continued. They'd rationed their energy carefully, knowing that conserving their strength during storms like this was just as important as the physical exertion of climbing.

Paul eventually took it upon himself to make the best meal they had so far: jalapeño poppers.

They had packed fresh produce and frozen food, opting for quality meals despite the extra weight. Wrapped in bacon and stuffed with cream cheese, the jalapeños sizzled in the small vestibule of the tent, the savory smell rising into the cold air and lifting their spirits.

For a few minutes, the storm faded into background noise. The tent transformed into something warmer, more human, not just shelter, but a place of comfort.

"This is going to hit the spot," Brandon said, his face lit up with anticipation.

"Best decision we've made so far," Paul replied, focused on the tiny pan. The hiss of grease in the cold air was the closest thing to joy any of them had felt in hours.

Mark leaned closer, inhaling the scent of jalapeños, bacon, and cream cheese like it was a campfire. "Who knew we'd be eating like kings on Denali?"

"We're doing all right," Brandon said, stretching his legs out a little. "Honestly, this makes the wind sound less... hostile."

Outside, the storm was unrelenting: a white roar against fabric walls. But inside, it was almost peaceful. The food, the laughter, and the stories reminded them they were still themselves out here. Still whole.

They did not talk much after the meal. They did not need to. Just the occasional comment about the wind's pitch or a shared glance when the tent shuddered.

At one point, the silence between them deepened, not heavy, but grounded. It was the quiet of people who trusted each other completely. A team not just climbing the same mountain but carrying each other through it.

Paul checked the weather again as the final weather fax image came through. The storm had stalled: thick cloud cover spinning stubbornly in place. "Still stuck," he said flatly.

Mark did not look surprised. "We wait."

Brandon yawned. "We wait. We eat poppers. We survive."

They all chuckled, but no one said more. They zipped into their bags, listening as the wind pulled at the walls like a thing alive.

This was not sleep. Not yet. Just the long stillness before whatever came next.

The wind clawed at the tent, but inside, they held fast, three breaths in the dark, waiting for the mountain to decide.

CHAPTER FIVE

Into the Heart of the Mountain

The next morning, the storm had passed, leaving behind a brilliant, cloudless sky that stretched endlessly over the snow-covered landscape. As the early light filtered into their tent, Mark was the first to stir, brushing off the thin layer of frost that had gathered on the edges of his sleeping bag. The quiet outside, after hours of relentless wind, felt almost unnatural. He rubbed his eyes and sat up, adjusting to the morning's stillness.

"Look at that," Brandon murmured, still wrapped in his sleeping bag but watching something through the small window of the tent.

Mark turned to see what had captured Brandon's attention. A lone bird, black against the vast whiteness, hovered just outside their tent, curious about the strange object that had appeared in its frozen world. Mark smiled at the sight, finding it oddly comforting in the otherwise harsh and desolate environment.

"The first bit of life we've seen in days," Mark said quietly.

Paul, already halfway out of his sleeping bag, nodded in agreement. "Take it as a good omen."

The team rose and began their morning routine. Their gear was mostly fine, just lightly covered by the snowfall from the storm.

Their packs were half-buried in the snow, but nothing had frozen or malfunctioned. Mark dug out the stove and soon had water boiling from freshly melted snow. The smell of hot coffee filled the tent as they prepared for the day's push toward Camp 2 and beyond.

Once packed up and ready, they stepped out into the beautiful sunny day. The landscape, now calm, was a stark contrast to the chaos of the earlier storm. Everything was still. The snow beneath their feet crunched softly as they began their ascent, the mountain bathed in a crisp white light. The distant rumble of avalanches echoed faintly, a reminder that even on a day like this, Denali was still unpredictable.

By midmorning, the team had passed Camp 2 without stopping. The weather remained in their favor, and the smoothness of the terrain allowed them to keep a steady pace. The mountain, now under the gentle warmth of the sun, was both beautiful and menacing. They had been isolated for days, moving steadily upward through storms and tough terrain. But today, Denali seemed to offer a reprieve.

It was near the base of Motorcycle Hill that they encountered other climbers for the first time since leaving Base Camp. As they approached the camp, they spotted a small group setting up tents. Mark led the way as they approached, and the distant figures soon came into focus.

Among the group was Chad, a climber who looked to be in his mid-forties, with a sun-weathered face that spoke of years spent in harsh conditions. He turned and smiled as they approached, offering a friendly nod.

"First time on Denali?" Chad asked, his voice warm and welcoming.

Mark shook his head. "First time for me, but we've all had our share of climbs."

Chad grinned. "Well, you picked a good one. This place has a way of humbling even the most experienced. Climbed it once before, a few years back."

"You've been up here before?" Mark asked, impressed.

"Yeah," Chad said, pulling his pack tighter. "Summited on a perfect day, just like this one. I couldn't resist coming back for more."

They exchanged pleasantries for a while, swapping stories about past climbs. Chad's confidence and knowledge of the mountain were evident, but he wasn't boastful. He seemed genuinely happy to be back on Denali, and his enthusiasm was infectious. As they set up their camp nearby, there was a sense of shared experience, even if they were from different teams.

Later that evening, Mark, Paul, and Brandon sat together in their cook tent. The plan for the following day was straightforward: cache their food at the 14,000-foot camp, then return to the base of Motorcycle Hill to rest and prepare for the next leg of the climb.

While Mark outlined their expected timeline, Paul rummaged through his pack again with growing frustration.

Brandon glanced over. "Still hoping the spork magically appears?"

Paul zipped the last compartment shut and sat back with a sigh. "It's gone. I've torn this pack apart three times. Either it never made it out of Talkeetna, or it disappeared."

Mark raised an eyebrow. "The spork?"

Paul nodded. "Yeah. I'm officially utensil-less."

Brandon tossed over his knife. "You and that knife are starting to have a real thing. You're going to owe it its own summit photo at this rate."

They chuckled, the ease between them a small victory after the mountain's earlier challenges.

The mood was light as they ate a simple meal, the air outside calm and clear. They hadn't felt this relaxed since leaving Base Camp, and the interaction with the other climbers, especially Chad, had added a new dimension to the journey. For the first time, they felt the camaraderie that came from knowing others were sharing the same mountain, the same challenges.

After the meal, they sat in the tent, talking quietly, the warmth of their bodies and the stove providing a comforting respite from the cold outside. It had been a good day, and the prospect of making progress in the morning lifted their spirits even more.

△ △ △

The next morning, the team set out early. The weather remained perfect, the skies a brilliant blue with no sign of the storm that had hounded them before. They began their ascent toward the cache site, moving steadily up the steep incline of Motorcycle Hill.

It was mid-climb, near the top of Motorcycle Hill, when, without warning, the ground beneath Brandon gave way.

He had unclipped just minutes earlier, judging the terrain flat enough to be safe. But Denali didn't care about confidence.

Paul saw him drop without a sound.

One moment Brandon was walking on solid snow. The next instance, the surface gave way and he plunged straight down. His feet vanished first, then his legs, hips, chest, and finally his head, swallowed by the glacier before Paul could shout his name.

Paul's stomach dropped as if he had fallen too.

"Mark! Brandon fell into a crevasse!" Paul shouted, his voice sharp, urgent. Paul reached instinctively for his axe but froze. Brandon had been off the rope.

Mark didn't rush. The sound of snow crunching underfoot and the eerie silence that followed left a chill even colder than the air. Mark knew a single misstep could make things worse. Staying clipped into Paul, he cautiously approached the area, stopping several feet from the fragile edge of the crevasse. "Brandon! Can you hear me?" he called out, careful not to disturb the unstable snow.

A moment passed before Brandon's voice echoed faintly from below. "Yeah, I'm okay! I hit a ledge about 10 feet down. I got an ice screw in."

Relief swept through them. Brandon was safe for now but still stuck inside the crevasse. Mark exchanged a glance with Paul, and the two nodded, understanding the urgency of the situation.

Two female researchers from another climbing team approached quickly, seeing the commotion. Together, they devised a plan. Paul anchored the group while Mark and the researchers set up a rescue system.

Mark called down to Brandon. "We're sending the rope down to you now. Just hang tight."

Brandon's voice came back, steadier than before. "Got it. I'm ready."

Paul held the line firm while the rest of the group worked to pull Brandon up. It took time, but eventually, Brandon's helmet appeared at the edge of the crevasse. Mark reached out and grabbed onto his pack, pulling him safely back onto solid ground.

Brandon coughed as Mark yanked him up. His first breath was loud, grateful.

"Next time," Mark said, grinning as he pulled the rope free, "just say you're tired. No need for theatrics."

Brandon laughed, weakly but genuinely. "Ten out of ten for drama, right?"

Paul exhaled and said, "Let's keep the stunts to a minimum from here on out."

For a few seconds, no one spoke, just standing there watching their breath cloud and drift together in the biting cold. A smile slowly spread across Mark's face, and when Brandon caught it, he couldn't help but mirror it with a relieved grin of his own. The gravity of what had just happened hung in the air between them, a sobering reminder of just how quickly things could turn.

Brandon's hands shook as he brushed the snow from his gear. He didn't speak right away, just stared at the void where the mountain had opened beneath him. It was as if part of him was still down there. He cautiously moved over and sat down where Paul was for a moment, breathing deeply. His face was pale, but he wasn't panicking. The shock of the fall had shaken him, but he gathered himself quickly, still shaken by the experience.

"That was...close," Brandon said, his voice slightly shaky but composed. "Didn't even see it coming."

Paul, still holding the line secure, gave a small smile. "That ledge saved you."

Brandon nodded, still taking deep breaths, though he was beginning to calm down. "Yeah, no kidding. I'm good now."

Mark clapped a hand on his shoulder. "You trying to get your name on a plaque up here?"

Brandon let out a shaky laugh. "Guess I like making an entrance."

Paul shook his head, his expression tight with residual adrenaline. "Let's not make that a habit."

After a short rest, Paul carefully marked the crevasse so other climbers would know to avoid it. The team then cached their supplies at the top of Motorcycle Hill, short of what they had planned. Brandon, though still a bit rattled, wasn't overwhelmed by the experience. The group finished their work and began the descent back to camp.

Back at camp that evening, the team huddled inside the cook tent. The warm air and the smell of pizza and brownies filled the space, creating a comforting atmosphere after the tension of the day.

Brandon seemed quieter than usual, not withdrawn, just inward. Like someone still hearing the echo of something that had passed too close. He took a long breath through his nose, eyes flicking toward the stove where the brownies were cooling, then down to the pizza in his hands. His fingers were steady again.

"You know," he said, picking at a slice of pizza, "I don't think I'm ever walking near you two without checking the snow first."

Mark smirked. "That's the spirit. Trust issues are how we know we're serious climbers."

Paul raised an eyebrow. "Says the guy who once walked off a cornice in Colorado."

"Unfair. That was... partially snow's fault," Mark replied.

They all laughed, and the air loosened around them, like a knot finally giving.

Mark noticed Chad lingering nearby and waved him over. "Chad, come on in! We've got plenty," he said, motioning him toward the stove.

Chad entered, shaking off the cold and sitting down next to the group. "Heard about the crevasse," Chad said, giving a nod toward Brandon. "You all handled that well."

Mark glanced at Brandon, then nodded. "Yeah. It wasn't what we expected, but we were prepared."

Brandon laughed lightly, though there was still a hint of tension in his voice. "It happened fast. One second I was walking, and then I fell. Looking down from that ledge, I couldn't see the bottom. Just blackness. Miles deep, it felt like. I got lucky. I'm still shaken, but I'll be fine."

Chad smiled. "That's Denali. You think you've got everything under control, and it throws something unexpected at you. That's why we respect it, and why we're all here, challenging ourselves to push through."

As the evening went on, the mood lightened. Brandon's shaken state gradually gave way to his usual demeanor, and by the time they finished their meal, the day's events felt distant.

The cook tent buzzed with conversation, stories, and laughter as the team relaxed.

The rich warmth of melted cheese and fresh-baked brownies lingered in the air: a simple luxury that melted away the day's tension.

The challenges of the day were behind them. Tomorrow, they would continue their climb to 14,000-Foot Camp.

For now, they rested, not because it was over but because they were ready for what came next. The mountain would test them again. And when the mountain asked more of them, as it always would, they would be ready together.

CHAPTER SIX

A Life on the Line

T he night before the push to the 14,000-foot camp, the signs had begun to show. Chad, usually steady and strong, had grown quiet after dinner. His breathing had become labored, and though his team had noticed, they attributed it to the altitude. But later, when his cough deepened and blood appeared, concern turned to alarm. They knew that something was seriously wrong.

Paul, Mark, and Brandon were camped nearby, unaware of Chad's worsening condition. The night passed quietly, with only the occasional distant roar of an avalanche breaking the stillness. By morning, the air was crisp and the sky was clear. It was the perfect day for pushing higher toward the summit.

Mark, Paul, and Brandon began breaking down their camp, eager to make their way to 14,000-Foot Camp.

As Mark secured his gear, one of Chad's climbing partners approached, his face drawn with worry. "Mark," he said quietly, pulling him aside, "we've got a problem. It's Chad. He's not doing well. His breathing is getting worse, and he's coughing up blood. We've decided he needs to descend."

Mark's stomach clenched. HAPE, or High-Altitude Pulmonary Edema, is a potentially life-threatening condition, especially at these altitudes. He knew immediately that Chad's descent couldn't wait.

Mark stepped closer to the tent. "How many of you are going with him?"

"Just the two of us," Chad's teammate replied. "But honestly, we're not sure that's enough. If something goes wrong on the descent, we'll need another strong pair of hands."

Mark nodded slowly. "Three people to manage a descent with a compromised climber. Yeah... that makes sense."

"I'll talk to the others," Mark said, nodding quickly. He turned and walked over to where Brandon was packing up gear, his mind already spinning.

"Brandon, we've got a situation with Chad," Mark said, his voice serious.

Brandon looked up, concern flashing across his face. "What's going on?"

Mark quickly explained Chad's worsening condition: the blood in his cough, and the decision by his team that he needed to descend immediately. Brandon listened intently, processing the severity of the situation.

"So, what do we do?" Brandon asked.

Mark paused, glancing toward where Paul was still focused on breaking down camp. "We need to talk to Paul," he said, his voice heavy with the weight of what was coming.

A minute later, the two of them approached Paul, who was busy securing gear, unaware of the storm quietly unfolding beside their camp.

"Paul, we need to talk," Mark said, his voice low but urgent.

Paul stopped what he was doing, his attention fully on them. "What's going on?"

"Chad's in bad shape," Mark began. "He's coughing up blood, and his team says it's been getting worse overnight. They've decided he needs to descend, but they need help."

Paul's face darkened with concern as the situation became clear. He had seen signs of altitude sickness before, but this sounded much more serious. Blood in the lungs was a red flag. It wasn't just fatigue or altitude headaches. It was HAPE, and it is life-threatening.

Brandon spoke next, his voice steady but concerned. "They need a healthy climber to go down with them. They are asking for help."

Mark nodded. "Paul, we know this isn't an easy decision. You're not outside your element, but this is a tough call to make."

In the space between their words, Paul's mind unraveled.

Would he take the out if it were offered freely? A small part of him, dulled by exhaustion and uncertainty, almost whispered yes. But this wasn't the time. He was still strong. Stronger than ever, even. The climb up Motorcycle Hill hadn't left him winded. His legs were strong, his lungs clear. He had felt something close to joy during that stretch, not just endurance, but flow. This was supposed to be the part where everything started to click, the stretch of the climb that shifted from hardship to grace.

He glanced at Mark. This was Mark's mountain. His summit to claim. Paul knew that. Mark had come here with something to prove for himself, something to heal. Paul and Brandon had come to support him, not to reach the summit at any cost, but to help him find whatever it was he had lost.

Mark couldn't go down. Not now.

If Brandon went down, the team would be off balance. He was the stronger climber for Mark on the upper mountain. If anyone was going to stay with Mark, it needed to be him.

Paul had plenty of first aid training over the years, enough experience to keep an eye on Chad and respond if his condition worsened. If someone had to descend with an injured climber, it had to be Paul.

The mountain had been everything he hoped it would be: challenging, beautiful, even fun. It wasn't supposed to end like this. Not yet.

Still, thoughts had a way of turning on you out here. You started wondering if your steps were slower than the others, if you were dragging the team down. He shook those doubts off.

This wasn't doubt. It was decision.

He could always come back. He would come back.

But Chad might not get another chance.

Paul's gaze lingered on the distant summit, the last stretch of the climb they'd worked so hard for. A pang of regret twisted inside him, the pull of the summit sharper than the cold air pressing against his skin. They had trained for this, prepared for this, and now they were almost there, just a week away from their goal. But now, a different kind of challenge had presented itself, and Paul knew what was at stake. The dream he had worked for was slipping through his fingers, and the weight of the decision pressed down hard on him. He breathed deeply, steadying himself as the decision crystallized. It would haunt him for years to come, he knew, but this was a different kind of ascent.

The silence stretched between them, the cold mountain air wrapping around them as Paul stood motionless, eyes still fixed on the peak. He could feel the pull of the summit, but there was no escaping the reality in front of him.

Mark and Brandon met his gaze, a silent understanding passing between them. No words were needed; they knew what this meant for Paul, and in their brief exchange, Paul found the strength to move forward, knowing his friends were behind him in every way that mattered.

Finally, Paul took a deep breath, the decision made in his heart. "I'll go. I'll help him down."

Mark and Brandon nodded in understanding. The three of them had started this climb together, but now Paul's path was taking a different turn. It wasn't an easy choice, but it was the right one.

The plan solidified quickly, but each step felt heavy with unspoken thoughts. Paul knew that once they started down, there was no going back, not to the summit and not to the journey they'd set out on together. As he gripped his poles and prepared to descend with Chad's team, the finality of the choice settled in.

Paul pulled his small handheld radio out from his chest pocket and showed it to Mark.

"Two-Meter National Simplex," Paul said firmly. "Daily check-in. Seven P.M. after the weather update."

Paul added, slipping the radio back into his jacket pocket. "We both have our license. Let's put them to good use."

Mark nodded in reply. "Range back to Talkeetna should be good if we keep a clear line of sight."

"We'll make it work," Paul said. "We're still a team, even if I'm below the clouds."

Before they parted ways, Mark, Paul, and Brandon paused for one last moment as a team together. Standing side by side, they took in the enormity of the mountain surrounding them. Paul knew this might be the last time the three of them stood together on Denali. They took a few pictures together, hugged, and exchanged a few words before Paul clipped into the new rope line, ready to begin the descent with Chad's team.

Chad stood outside his tent, bundled up and clearly struggling but determined. His team had packed his bags, though Chad still carried them down himself. His breath came hard, but he pressed on, leaning heavily on his trekking poles.

As the group began their descent, Paul glanced back up the slope. Mark and Brandon remained at camp, small figures against the vast white. He lifted a hand in one final wave. Mark returned it. Then the slope turned, and they vanished from view.

Further down, Paul, Chad, and the team crossed paths with a park ranger and a medically trained volunteer making their way up. They exchanged a few words, just enough to inform the ranger of the marked crevasse on motorcycle hill and Chad's condition. The ranger and medic continued their climb, trusting the group to manage their self-evacuation.

Paul matched his steps to Chad's. Every few steps, he exchanged a glance in Chad's direction, helping signal their pace and keeping an eye on his breathing. Each pause in the march felt longer. Chad was making it down, but he was in pain.

For a while, the descent seemed manageable, though slow. Chad's breathing was labored, but he pushed through, supported by the team.

However, about halfway down the slope, near Camp 1, Chad's condition took a turn for the worse. He came to a sudden stop, gripping his trekking poles, his face twisted in pain. The effort of every breath was clear on his face. He hunched over, gasping, unable to move any further.

"My left arm has gone completely numb," he cried out.

He took a few more steps. In agony, Chad looked up in pain, his voice raw but firm. "You either call for a Park Ranger right now, or I press the SOS button."

No one hesitated. One of Chad's climbing partners immediately grabbed the radio and called for help. The Park Ranger and medic, now over an hour ahead of them, were contacted and began making their way back down the mountain to assist.

△ △ △

The team found a spot to rest while they waited. Chad sat down; his breathing heavy but still stable. His oxygen levels weren't normal, but they hadn't plummeted either. His heart rate was rapid, his body straining to keep up with the altitude.

Paul stayed close, speaking calmly to Chad to keep him alert. "Chad, I need you to focus. What's your name? Age? Any medical allergies?"

Chad responded, clearly in pain but responsive.

They monitored his vitals as they waited, logging his oxygen levels, heart rate, and breathing rate, trying to keep him as comfortable as possible while they waited for help. The minutes felt long, but Paul continued to check in, ensuring Chad stayed conscious and aware of his surroundings.

When the Park Ranger and medic finally returned, they assessed Chad's condition and all the notes that were taken from when his team stopped. After evaluating everything, it was clear he needed to be airlifted immediately. They called in for an airlift from their current position.

The Denali National Parks helicopter arrived at Camp 1 to transport Chad to Base Camp. Paul, the Park Ranger, medic, and another climber all worked together to load Chad onto the stretcher, securing him for the flight down. As the helicopter prepared for takeoff, Paul realized that some of his own gear had gone with Chad.

After the helicopter lifted off, Paul spoke with the park ranger about retrieving his gear. The ranger assured him that when the helicopter returned to pick her up, Paul would be able to get his belongings back. The park ranger also informed Chad's team that they needed to continue to Base Camp to get word if they were authorized to continue the climb or had to leave the mountain.

As the sound of the helicopter faded into the distance, the camp fell silent again, the crisis momentarily behind them.

The group decided to set up camp for the night, exhausted from the day's events. They would descend to Base Camp in the morning.

That night, the sky over Denali was breathtaking. The mountain glowed under the midnight sun, serene and beautiful, a stark contrast to the tension earlier in the day. Paul stepped out of the tent with his camera.

The mountain stood silent, untouched by the day's drama, the lighting casting golden streaks across its snow-draped ridges. Denali was unmoved, a silent witness to their struggles. As Paul clicked the shutter, he felt both small and strangely complete, a moment of stillness against the mountain's eternity. He felt a strange sense of closure. Even if his climb had ended differently than he had imagined, he would carry this memory with him, frozen in stillness, a moment so quiet and complete he wished it could last forever.

CHAPTER SEVEN

The Weight of Absence

Mark awoke to a muted stillness that felt heavier than the air inside the tent. He blinked against the early light filtering through the thin fabric, and, for a moment, he had to remind himself that Paul wasn't there. The familiar rustling of gear, the low hum of Paul's voice giving some last-minute weather update. Those sounds were gone now, replaced by a quiet emptiness. It struck him how, from now on, they'd be carrying more than just physical weight; they'd be carrying Paul's spirit with them, honoring the climb they'd started together. He had known this moment was coming since the night before, but waking up to an empty space where his brother had once been hit harder than expected.

Across from him, Brandon was sitting up, already in the midst of securing his sleeping bag for the day. They exchanged a wordless glance, both understanding what the other felt. With Paul no longer beside them, the climb would feel different. Yet, there was no time to dwell on it. They had their next challenge in front of them.

"I guess we should reassess everything today," Mark finally said, his voice a little rough from the frigid air. He rubbed his hands together, reaching for the stove to get some water boiling. "Make sure we're good to go without Paul."

Brandon nodded, his face set in quiet determination. "Yeah, better to figure that out here before we push on."

Paul, meanwhile, had found his own way back to Talkeetna. Paul and Mark's dad met Paul at the lodge and took him in without hesitation: warm meals, a roof, and quiet solidarity. He was not just waiting for his sons to come down off the mountain; he was in Talkeetna ready to provide logistical support in any way he could.

Mark and Brandon had made the decision the night before to spend an extra day at Motorcycle Hill. With Paul no longer with them, there were adjustments to be made: redistribution of gear, recalculating rations, and mentally preparing for the next leg of the climb. This wasn't something they could rush into. Mark was meticulous, but even he felt the unease gnawing at him. The climb had changed, and now they had to adapt.

The day stretched out slowly, filled with tasks that would have once felt routine, but now seemed heavier with meaning. They carefully went through their packs, checking and rechecking each piece of gear. There was no room for error.

Paul's departure meant more than just fewer hands to carry the load. It meant they needed to be doubly sure everything was accounted for.

Meanwhile, Paul wasted no time turning his attention to their communication lifeline. With their dad's help, he spent hours scouring the hills around Talkeetna, searching for high vantage points where the signal might punch through the static of distance and terrain. The two of them were a quiet, determined duo: building the antenna, mapping line-of-sight corridors, and testing connections with the same care and focus Mark and Brandon brought to the route ahead.

By mid-morning, the wind had started to pick up. It wasn't anything aggressive yet, just a reminder that Denali was always watching, always testing. They moved with quiet efficiency, dividing Paul's share of the gear and food, and discussing their strategy for the upcoming ascent. Though neither said it aloud, there was a mutual understanding: from here on, they had to rely on each other in ways they hadn't before. It wasn't just about physical endurance; it was about trust.

Mark ran his fingers over the edge of the map they had brought, eyes scanning the route they would take in the coming days. "We've got enough supplies for the push," he said, more to himself than to Brandon. "But we can't afford any mistakes. Weather's unpredictable up here."

Brandon glanced up from securing the stove, his breath visible in the chilly air. "We'll be fine," he said, though his tone carried more determination than certainty. "We've done tough climbs before."

Mark nodded, but the tension lingered. This wasn't like the other climbs. This was Denali.

When everything was packed, they paused for only a moment, then turned toward the next stretch of mountain.

The wind had become a steady presence, a low whistle that echoed across the slopes. Clouds were thickening overhead as they turned toward the next stretch of mountain. It wasn't brutal yet, but the cold bit at their fingers through their gloves, and Mark knew they would need to stay alert.

The first few hours of the climb were manageable, the wind pushing against them but not yet strong enough to slow them down significantly. But as they gained altitude, the gusts became sharper, cutting through their layers and making each step a little harder. The familiar feeling of numbness started to creep into their fingers and toes, and they stopped frequently to check for signs of frostbite.

They had faced cold before, but this was different. Denali's cold was a living thing, wrapping around them and testing their resilience. Mark's mind wandered back to Paul for a moment, wondering what he would think of the conditions today. Paul's technical mind would be calculating the drop in temperature, checking wind speeds, and formulating a plan. Mark took comfort in the thought. Paul wasn't physically with them, but his presence was still felt in the decisions they made.

△ △ △

As they pressed forward, the landscape around them shifted, and soon they found themselves approaching a familiar stretch of terrain. The crevasse. Brandon's pace slowed the moment he saw the two wands crossed in the shape of an X, marking the place where Paul had warned other climbers to steer clear a few days before. He didn't need to look at the crevasse itself. The memory of that fall, the air rushing past him, was enough.

His breath hitched, and for a brief moment, he was back in that terrifying moment: the split second when the snow gave way and he landed on the narrow ledge below. The surge of adrenaline came rushing back as he remembered clawing himself to a stop before he could slide any farther into the crevasse.

Mark must have noticed the change in his pace. He glanced over his shoulder, concern in his eyes as he followed Brandon's gaze toward the wands.

"You all right?" Mark asked, his voice barely audible over the wind.

Brandon nodded slowly, his gaze fixed on the crevasse. "Yeah, just remembering...how close it was." His fingers involuntarily tightened around his trekking poles, a chill crawling up his spine as he recalled the fall: the sudden rush of air, the sickening drop, and the terrifying emptiness beneath him.

Mark gave a solemn nod. He hadn't seen Brandon fall, but he had seen what it left behind: the shaken look in his friend's eyes and the silence that followed. Standing here now, just feet from the spot, the weight of it returned like the cold biting at their faces.

With a shared, unspoken understanding, they moved on. The memory remained behind them, buried but not forgotten, like so much on this mountain.

△ △ △

When they reached 14,000-Foot Camp, the change in atmosphere was palpable. High on the mountain, 14,000-Foot Camp was like a second Base Camp, busy with climbers waiting for their opportunity to push higher. A small village of colorful tents dotted the snow, a stark contrast to the endless white that surrounded them. Climbers wandered between tents, cooking meals, repairing gear, or simply standing in silence, staring out at the breathtaking views that stretched in every direction.

Despite being so high, life at 14,000-Foot Camp felt peaceful. There was a sense of serenity that Mark and Brandon hadn't expected. The camp bustled with activity, yet there was an unspoken stillness, a shared understanding that patience was essential. Everyone was waiting for the right weather window, knowing it could take days or even weeks before they could safely climb to 17,000-Foot Camp.

Late one afternoon, a low drumming sound rolled over the camp. Everyone recognized it. Mark unzipped the tent and stepped outside, shielding his eyes against the bright glare off the snow. A helicopter crested the ridge, flying slow, its path sweeping across the shoulder of the mountain.

Brandon joined him, squinting up at the sky.

"They don't come for nothing," he said.

All around the camp, climbers had paused what they were doing. Conversations fell silent. Snow saws were set down. Heads tilted toward the sound. The mood shifted without anyone saying a word.

The aircraft hovered high above the slope, circling once before descending slowly toward Denali Pass, a dangerous traverse at over 18,000 feet. The kind of place where even one misstep could be fatal.

It didn't take long to spot the line beneath the helicopter.

A single black sling dangled from the belly of the aircraft, swaying slightly in the downdraft. Suspended in it was a body bag, small from this distance, but unmistakable in shape and color.

No rescue. Just recovery.

Someone did not make it.

The rotors thudded as the helicopter banked southwest, carrying its cargo out of sight. Within moments, the camp was quiet again. The breeze returned. The snowfields glistened. Normal resumed.

But it was not the same.

Mark's gaze remained fixed on the ridge. "That was Denali Pass," he said, voice low. "Same section we'll be crossing."

Brandon didn't respond right away. His eyes were still on the sky where the chopper had disappeared.

Mark exhaled slowly. "On this mountain, sometimes one misstep is all you get."

They didn't speak after that. There was nothing left to say. Only the quiet hiss of the stove behind them, and the hollow silence Denali always left in its wake.

Mark and Brandon spent their days at 14,000-Foot Camp checking their gear, melting snow, and sharing stories with other fellow climbers. There was a quiet camaraderie among the climbers, a recognition that they were all here for the same reason, facing the same challenges. It wasn't just about reaching the summit, but about surviving the mountain together.

"This place is something else," Brandon said, taking in the scene. "We'll miss it."

Mark nodded. "Yeah, even with everything...there's something about being up here."

Inside their tent, the air was still frigid, but the shelter provided a much-needed reprieve from the relentless wind. As they huddled in their sleeping bags, coaxing warmth back into their bodies, they finally allowed themselves to relax, just a little. For the first time since they'd left Motorcycle Hill, they could let go. The warmth of shared company filled the space, a quiet celebration of endurance as they let themselves be still for a moment.

Mark reached for the radio. The familiar crackle of static filled the tent. He pressed the button, his voice low but steady. "Paul, you there?"

Mark's shoulders ached from the day's climb, the cold working its way deep into his bones. After a moment, Paul's voice cracked through the static. "I'm here. How's it going up there?"

The sound of Paul's voice felt like a lifeline, a thread that connected them back to the person who had started this climb with them. Even though he was off the mountain now, his presence remained strong. Every call reinforced their sense of purpose and anchored them in the journey they'd begun together, grounding them in more than just weather updates. It was a reminder of the commitment they shared. This daily check-in was more than just a formality; it was a way of keeping Paul part of the team.

"We're good," Brandon said, though the fatigue was evident in his voice. "Made it to 14,000 feet. Wind's picking up, but we're managing."

"That's good to hear," Paul replied. "I've got weather updates for the next few days. It's not looking great, but you're in a good spot for now. I'll keep you updated."

The conversation was brief. Just facts, logistics, and updates. But in those short exchanges, there was a reassurance that went beyond words. Paul might be off the mountain, but he was still with them, guiding them from afar.

Then, after a short pause on the radio, Paul added, "By the way, remember that spork I swore I packed?"

Mark and Brandon exchanged a look.

"I found it," Paul said. "In Talkeetna. Packed in my luggage I left behind."

Despite the exhaustion, Mark and Brandon laughed. Even through the static, Mark could hear the smile in his brother's voice. The simple, ridiculous update somehow made the cold feel a little less sharp.

On nights when Paul could not check in, it was their dad's voice that came across the airwaves instead, briefed by Paul earlier that day, steady, factual, and always a little reserved, as though guarding his emotions behind barometric readings. But to Mark and Brandon, it meant everything. He had not climbed with them, but he was always in their corner, quietly anchoring their journey from Talkeetna.

After they signed off, Mark set the radio aside and leaned back, staring up at the roof of the tent. The wind outside had calmed slightly, though it still whistled through the camp, a constant reminder of where they were. They were tired, cold, and aching, but they had made it through another day.

"We're doing this," Mark said softly, more to himself than to Brandon, but his friend nodded in agreement.

They had made it this far, and with Paul and their dad still supporting them from a distance, they felt a renewed sense of determination. The summit wasn't far off now.

CHAPTER EIGHT

Higher Grounds

The wind outside their tent had finally calmed, a rare moment of stillness on the mountain. Mark and Brandon lay in their sleeping bags, the thin, frigid air inside the tent offering little warmth. They had grown accustomed to the cold by now, but there was no ignoring the ache in their muscles from days of waiting, watching, and bracing for the next move.

"We've been here longer than we expected," Brandon said, his voice breaking the morning silence.

Mark nodded, though his eyes remained focused on the ceiling of the tent. He'd been tracking their supplies each day, quietly calculating how much longer they could last here at 14,000-Foot Camp. The challenge wasn't just the mountain, it was the waiting. Climbing to High Camp wasn't something you could rush. You had to wait for Denali to give you the green light. And while the calm mornings and clear skies made the climb tempting, the signs weren't quite right just yet.

"Could be today though," Mark said. His voice carried the kind of calm certainty that had kept them moving forward all these years. "We'll wait and see how things look after breakfast."

Brandon sat up, already reaching for the stove. The routine of camp life had become second nature by now: checking gear, boiling snow for water, talking strategy while they ate. But today, there was a different kind of energy. They both felt it. The window might open soon, and with it, the chance to push for 17,000-Foot Camp.

In the days before, they had made sure to retrieve the cache they had left behind at the top of Motorcycle Hill. It had been a tough climb even without full packs, but the cache was crucial for their next push toward 17,000-Foot Camp because it contained extra food, fuel, and supplies. After camping at 14,000 feet, they returned to their cache, dug it out from beneath the packed snow, and secured it in their packs. Each small effort to gather what they had stored felt like another step toward the summit.

As Mark tallied their remaining food, each item took on added weight. They'd been watching their reserves dwindle slowly, like sand slipping through an hourglass. Each day at 14,000-Foot Camp was a slow duel between patience and dwindling supplies. If the mountain didn't allow a clear window soon, the scales would tip. He exchanged a quiet glance with Brandon, who seemed to understand the unspoken calculation. They were holding steady for now, but the days left at 14,000-Foot Camp were numbered.

△ △ △

By mid-morning, the sky had opened up, clear, blue, and endless. It was the kind of sky that every climber waited for, the kind that meant you didn't question the mountain's mood. You took advantage of it.

"Looks like we've got our window," Mark said, zipping up his jacket and stepping outside the tent. The cold bit at his face, but the absence of wind was a relief. This was the break they needed.

Breaking down camp was far from a quick process. It took nearly an hour to gather their gear, dismantle the tent, and pack everything tightly for the climb ahead. At this altitude, conserving energy was crucial, and rushing through anything could mean mistakes. The cold gnawed at their fingers as they stuffed their gear into their packs, but the excitement of finally moving forward kept them focused.

Brandon followed Mark as they made their way toward the fixed rope line running up the steep terrain that connected 14,000-Foot Camp to 17,000-Foot Camp. They clipped in, fastening their carabiners was automatic. The rope line was a lifeline on this part of the climb, a steady guide that would take them up the exposed ridge, where every step was a battle against gravity and altitude.

The trail to 17,000-Foot Camp climbed sharply, cutting across exposed ridgelines with nothing but wind and gravity on either side. Mark led the way. The altitude was higher now, and every step felt heavier, but he was in his element. The cold, thin air and the towering landscape all felt like part of him. Brandon followed just behind, his own breath coming in steady bursts as he matched Mark's pace. There was something both exhilarating and terrifying about being on the ridge, fully exposed to the elements. They were explorers again, pushing toward the summit with nothing but the mountain beneath them and the sky above.

△ △ △

The hours passed slowly as they ascended, but the skies remained clear, offering breathtaking views of the surrounding peaks. Mark paused occasionally, allowing Brandon to catch up, and they would exchange a few words about the climb, about the clear weather, and about the summit that now felt tantalizingly close.

"This is it," Brandon said during one such break, looking out over the horizon. "This is what we came for."

Mark nodded, taking in the view. "Almost there."

They didn't linger long. While the conditions were perfect for the ascent, they both knew the reality of high-altitude climbing. It was a game of patience and endurance.

As Mark adjusted the strap on his pack, he felt that ever-present tension beneath his breath, a subtle reminder that the mountain never truly relaxed its grip. Denali could give you moments of clarity, even beauty, but it always waited, watching. You had to move with respect, not ambition. That was how you stayed alive.

△ △ △

By the time they reached 17,000-Foot Camp, the sun had dipped slightly in the sky, casting long shadows across the snow-covered ridge. The climb had taken its toll, but they had made it. Exhaustion hit them both hard as they began searching for a suitable camping spot. The ground was hard-packed snow, uneven in places, but after a few minutes of searching, they found a spot that would provide shelter from the wind.

Once the tent was up and their gear was secured, they collapsed inside, both too tired to say much. Mark checked their supplies. The little they had left was stretched thin. They had enough to last a few more days, but it was clear that they couldn't afford any more delays. The summit push had to come soon.

High Camp, also known as 17,000-Foot Camp, was a surreal place. A scattering of tents dotted the otherwise barren, white expanse of snow and ice. The air was thin, biting at every breath. The altitude made even the simplest tasks feel monumental. Yet, here in this desolate space, life thrived. Climbers from all over the world huddled in their tents, waiting for the moment when they could make their final push. Despite the isolation, there was a sense of camaraderie, a quiet but unspoken bond between the teams who had made it this far. The knowledge that each person was experiencing the same physical and mental challenges created a unique sense of connection, even without words.

The atmosphere at 17,000-Foot Camp was different from the lower elevations. There were fewer climbers now, and the ones who were there knew the stakes. Supplies were limited at this height, and survival was a cooperative effort. At 14,000-Foot Camp, climbers were more independent, but here at 17,000-Foot Camp, there was a strong sense of camaraderie: a shared understanding that everyone was facing the same unforgiving conditions, and that getting through it meant helping one another.

They hadn't been at 17,000-Foot Camp long before a climber from the next tent emerged, bundled tightly, snow clinging to his jacket. He trudged over, holding a small packet in his hand. "Got some extra soup mix if you need it," he offered, his breath creating clouds between them.

Brandon accepted the packet with a tired grin. "Can't say no to that. Thanks." At this height, generosity wasn't a show of goodwill; it was essential. In the thin air and numbing cold, survival meant teamwork, and here at 17,000 feet, there was no room for ego. Even as strangers, they were a team.

The climber stayed for a few moments, exchanging stories of the climb so far and talking about the summit day ahead. The camaraderie was palpable. At 17,000-Foot Camp, pretenses fell away. This was about survival, about making sure everyone had the chance to reach the summit and, more importantly, make it back down safely.

"Everyone's on the same team up here," the other climber said with a small smile before heading back to his own tent.

"You don't see competition at this height, just people trying to help each other out."

Mark glanced at Brandon as they prepared to settle in for the night. "Makes a difference, doesn't it?"

Brandon smiled back, a rare flicker of light in his exhausted eyes. "Yeah. It really does."

△ △ △

Later that evening, after they had settled in, Mark turned on the radio to check in with Paul.

"Paul, you there?" Mark said, his voice low but steady as he adjusted the radio's frequency.

There was a brief crackle of static before Paul's voice came through, clear and reassuring. "I'm here. How's it looking up there?"

"We made it to 17,000-Foot Camp," Mark replied. "Weather's holding, and we're prepping for the summit push."

"That's great to hear," Paul said, his tone lifting slightly. "Be ready for high winds, but it looks like you'll have clear skies for the next day or two with better wind conditions two days from now. How's your food supply holding up?"

Mark hesitated for a moment before answering. "We're running low, but we've been able to share some with the other teams. We're all right for now."

Paul's voice grew more serious. "Just make sure you conserve as much as possible. The summit push is the longest day of the climb. You'll need all your energy for that."

"We know," Brandon chimed in, his voice tired but resolute. "We're ready."

After a few more exchanges, they signed off. As the radio fell silent, Mark felt the weight of the journey settle into his bones. Days of rationing, hours of freezing wind, and the relentless altitude had worn them down, body and mind. His muscles ached from the climb, each movement sending a reminder of their shared resilience.

△ △ △

As they settled into their sleeping bags, the frigid air pressing in around them, Mark and Brandon talked quietly about the final push. The summit was now within their grasp, but they knew better than to get ahead of themselves. Denali wasn't a mountain you rushed up. They would wait for another clear weather window, just as they had before. But there was a shared sense of urgency now. Their supplies wouldn't last forever, and the high winds Paul had mentioned could make things even harder.

"We've come this far," Mark said quietly, his breath visible in the frigid air. "Just one more push."

He didn't have to elaborate; Brandon knew. They both felt the toll, but neither would turn back now. They had endured the worst Denali had thrown their way. Now, after weeks of watching and waiting, the summit was near. In the distance, the summit rose beyond a frozen shoulder of ice, not yet close but no longer a dream.

CHAPTER NINE

The Summit in Sight

Mark stirred in his sleeping bag, the thin air doing little to alleviate the grogginess that came with another night at 17,000-Foot Camp. Every breath felt shallow, as though the mountain itself was pressing down on him, making it harder to pull air into his lungs. Across from him, Brandon sat up, already rubbing his face with gloved hands, his breath visible in the frigid air inside the tent.

"You get any sleep?" Brandon asked, his voice rough from the altitude.

Mark shook his head, letting out a long sigh. "Not much."

Brandon nodded, understanding the strain all too well. The altitude at 17,000-Foot Camp weighed on them both. The night had been a struggle, with the cold biting at their extremities and sleep coming only in short, restless bursts. Outside, the camp was quieter, more focused. Climbers who made it this far were preparing for the final push, each team intent on their own journey to the top.

Mark sat up, unzipping his sleeping bag. The air inside the tent was frigid, making every action feel slower. Supplies were running low, and they had barely enough for the summit push.

"We're cutting it close," he said, holding up the small pile of rations. "Just a few energy bars and a packet of freeze-dried soup." Each item felt woefully inadequate for what lay ahead. He wondered if it would be enough but banished the thought before it settled; they had come too far to turn back now.

Brandon glanced over, his face set in a look of determination. "It'll be enough," he said. "We'll make it last."

Mark was struck, not for the first time, by Brandon's quiet resolve; even as supplies dwindled, he held steady, confident they'd reach the summit.

They shared a sparse breakfast, eating in relative silence as they prepared for the long day ahead. The frigid air bit at their faces, and the food barely gave them the energy they needed. Other climbers moved around camp, preparing for their own summit pushes, some offering a quick nod or a few words of encouragement. Some climbers, noticing Mark and Brandon's low supplies, shared extra food with them. It wasn't much, just enough to keep them going for the next few days. Even so, the shared provisions made a world of difference. Up here, survival wasn't just about skill or strength; it was about relying on each other.

After their meal, Mark stepped outside to check the gear when Brandon's voice cut through the crisp morning air. "Hey, Mark, you've got to see this," he called from inside the tent.

Mark ducked back inside, his curiosity piqued. Brandon was holding up his phone, his eyes wide with surprise. "We've got a signal!"

Mark's brow furrowed as he moved closer. A faint, flickering signal appeared on the screen, just enough to send out a message. The sight brought a surge of unexpected warmth; a rare link to the outside world. Outside, the mountain stretched vast and indifferent, but here, with the signal, they were sons, brothers, friends, connected to the lives they had left behind.

Mark quickly texted his mom, just enough to say they had made it to 17,000-Foot Camp and were preparing for the summit push. Brandon sent a message to his family as well.

After a few minutes, the connection flickered out, leaving them once again alone with the mountain. But the brief contact had been enough. They had let their families know they were safe, and now it was time to focus on the climb ahead.

As the afternoon stretched on, the clear skies seemed to promise a perfect weather window for the summit push. Mark and Brandon knew they couldn't rush. The conditions had to be exactly right.

Over the next few days, they stayed at 17,000-Foot Camp, carefully rationing their supplies and relying on the generosity of the other climbers. The extra food shared with them helped stretch their rations, just enough to keep their energy up while waiting for the perfect window. There was a quiet determination shared among the climbers, each focused on their goal, knowing they would need patience and strength to make it to the summit.

Each day, they scanned the horizon for signs, hoping the clear skies and stillness would hold, but as Mark pulled out the radio that evening, it was with a cautious optimism. Weather could turn in an instant. They needed assurance from Paul that the mountain was truly ready to let them pass.

"Paul, you there?" he called into the radio.

Paul's voice came through, clearer than expected. "I'm here. How's it going up there?"

The warmth in his tone felt grounding, a steady line of connection, and in the chill of 17,000-Foot Camp, it was an anchor back to their starting point and all the planning that had brought them here.

"We're good. Supplies are low, but we're making it. What's the weather looking like?"

Paul's voice lifted slightly. "You're in luck. It looks perfect up there: clear skies and little to no wind. You couldn't ask for better conditions. And it looks like the forecast is good for the next few days."

Mark exchanged a glance with Brandon who nodded, the excitement evident in his eyes. This was it. The break they'd been waiting for. Paul continued with a few more updates, but the message was clear: if they wanted to make the push, now was the time.

"Thanks, Paul," Mark said, feeling the weight of anticipation settle over him. "We'll go tomorrow."

"Take your time and enjoy it," Paul said, his voice softer now. "You've earned it."

Mark and Brandon signed off, feeling the finality of their decision settle in. Tomorrow would be the day.

That evening, as they prepared for the summit, Mark couldn't help but reflect on how far they had come. The weeks spent on the mountain, the days of grueling altitude climbs, Paul's departure, the bone-deep cold. All had led to this moment. Each setback, each hardship, had forged them and given shape to why they were here. For Mark, reaching this point wasn't just a goal; it was the culmination of everything he had fought to reclaim.

"Tomorrow," Mark murmured, more to himself than to Brandon, though his friend nodded in agreement.

"We've got this," Brandon replied, the determination in his voice clear despite the exhaustion etched into his face.

They spent the night in relative silence, their minds focused on the climb. The altitude had taken its toll on them both, and with their diminished supplies, every movement felt heavier. But their determination had never wavered.

CHAPTER TEN

The Summit Push

The morning dawned frigid and quiet, a rare calm before their ultimate test. Mark and Brandon woke up early, shaking off the grogginess from the altitude. This was it. Mark knew it the moment he opened his eyes, the anticipation sharpening his senses in the stillness of the morning.

Beside him, Brandon was already moving, preparing for the summit push. They had slept fitfully, the altitude keeping them from deep rest, but adrenaline had begun to override the exhaustion.

"Ready?" Brandon asked in a muffled voice, glancing at Mark as he packed the last of his gear.

Mark nodded. "I was born ready!"

They moved with quiet efficiency, packing their daypacks with only what they needed for the final ascent: food, extra layers, and emergency supplies. Their packs were lighter, but every step would still feel monumental. The summit loomed above them, hidden in the early morning darkness, but its pull was undeniable.

As they stepped out of the tent, the cold hit them fully. It was a biting, bone-deep cold, but the skies were clear and the wind was still. Paul's weather report from the previous night had been perfect. No storms. No wind. Nothing but a clear path to the summit.

Mark checked the rope lines one more time, making sure they were securely clipped in, knowing that up here, even the smallest mistake could be fatal. He looked over at Brandon, who gave a firm nod. "Yeah. Let's do this."

With a final glance back at 17,000-Foot Camp, they set off. Each step up the slope felt like leaving part of themselves behind: their fears, doubts, and the comfort of 17,000-Foot Camp. They were no longer just climbers but explorers, standing on the edge of their own limits, ready to carve the final steps toward the summit.

As the morning stretched on, the sun began to rise, casting a pale light across the snow-covered slopes. The landscape around them was breathtaking, the vast expanse of Denali unfolding beneath their feet. But neither Mark nor Brandon could focus on the beauty; their minds were locked on the climb, on the next step, and the one after that.

As they ascended, the path grew increasingly dangerous. Ice patches glinted underfoot, and the incline grew steeper, but they navigated each obstacle with practiced skill. The altitude was unforgiving, gnawing at their energy reserves, but they continued moving, taking short breaks to catch their breath, adjusting their gear and ropes when needed, always mindful of the dangers that lurked in the snow and ice around them.

As they neared a particularly steep section, a faint hum reached their ears, carried on the thin air. Mark paused, his eyes scanning the sky. "You hear that?"

Brandon stopped beside him, nodding. "Yeah...the plane."

They both knew who it was. Paul had told them he'd be flying over today, checking on their progress from the air. They squinted upward, and sure enough, in the distance, they saw the airplane circling above the summit. Paul was up there. Mark and Brandon felt a rush of gratitude. Paul had been a steady hand guiding them from afar, and now he was a part of this moment as much as they were.

Mark smiled to himself, knowing Paul would be looking down at their slow but steady progress. He knew Paul would try to contact them, but for now, they kept their radios off, conserving battery for when they reached the top. They waved briefly at the plane, a small acknowledgment of their brother and friend who had been with them every step of this journey, even if from a distance.

As they climbed higher, the summit came into view, but it still felt distant, as if the mountain was taunting them with how close they were yet how much more effort it would take to reach it. The final push to the summit was brutal. Every step felt like a battle, their bodies screaming for rest, their minds hazy from the altitude. But the summit was there, just ahead, and the thought of it pulled them forward.

Mark's legs felt heavy, as though the mountain itself was trying to hold him back, but he pushed through the exhaustion, focused on the goal. The years of preparation, the months of planning, the weeks of climbing had all led to this.

Finally, after what felt like an eternity, they reached it. The summit.

It was 6:44 p.m. on May 28, 2022. The sun hung low but unrelenting, casting long golden rays across the upper reaches of the mountain.

The thin, biting air felt like ice with each breath, but to Mark it was cleaner, sharper, a reminder of the freedom he had fought so hard to reclaim. The climb had brought him here, but the journey began long before Denali. Each step had peeled away the shadows of doubt, revealing a purpose he'd thought he'd lost.

Mark's breath caught in his throat as he took in the view, the vast expanse of North America spread out below them. It was as though the world had stopped, suspended in a moment of pure, overwhelming clarity. The air was thinner than ever, but it felt lighter now, like a weight had been lifted from his chest.

Beside him, Brandon let out a breathless laugh, shaking his head in disbelief. "We did it."

Not long ago, Mark had doubted he'd ever walk without pain, let alone climb again. He remembered the weight of the brace, the grueling rehab, the dark mornings when progress felt impossible. And now, he stood above it all.

Mark smiled, his eyes wide as he looked around at the endless sky, the snow-covered peaks stretching out in every direction. They stood at the highest point in North America, and for a moment, nothing else existed.

Time seemed to stand still on the summit. The cold was biting, and the wind tugged at their jackets, but they didn't care. Mark and Brandon took in the view, the silence of the world around them more profound than they had ever experienced. The vastness of it all was humbling. They had worked so hard to reach this point, and now that they were here, it felt as though they were suspended between the earth and the sky, the only two people in the world.

They pulled out their cameras, snapping pictures of the landscape, of each other, and of the flags they had brought to the top. Every photo felt like it captured not just the moment, but the journey that had brought them here. The cold seeped into their bones, but they lingered longer than they should have, unable to pull themselves away from the beauty of the summit.

Mark gently pulled out the radio from his pack, his fingers numb from the cold. He adjusted the frequency, the static filling the air before he pressed the button. "Paul, you there?" His voice crackled into the silence.

A pause. Then, Paul's voice came through, faint but clear. "I'm here. How's it looking from up there?"

Mark grinned, glancing over at Brandon, who was still taking in the view. "It's...unreal. We're at the summit."

There was a crackle of static, then a second voice came through, deeper and holding back emotion.

"Proud of you, son!"

It was Dad, speaking from Talkeetna beside Paul.

"Thanks, Dad," Mark replied quickly, his throat tightening.

A brief silence followed, too cold for more.

Paul's laugh echoed through the radio. "I knew you'd make it. How's it feel?"

"Cold," Brandon chimed in, his breath visible in the thin air.

Mark chuckled, his breath catching in his chest. "It feels...-like everything. We did it, Paul!"

"I'm proud of you guys," Paul said, his voice thick with emotion. "Take it in. You earned this."

For a few minutes, they all stood there, connected by the faint radio signal, sharing in the triumph. It wasn't just Mark and Brandon's victory. It belonged to all of them, even from afar.

Before they signed off, Mark used the amateur radio to send a message to an operator in Anchorage. The operator relayed the message to Mark's mom, letting her know they had made it. The brief connection between the summit and home was a finishing touch to the accomplishment, as if they were bringing their families with them to the top.

As they stood at the summit, Mark's mind drifted back to the journey that had brought him here. It wasn't just the climb up Denali. It was the recovery after his accident, the years of pushing his body to heal, the emotional toll that had nearly broken him. He had felt lost, adrift without a purpose.

But this climb, this moment, was what he had been searching for.

The wind tugged at his jacket, the cold biting into his skin, but Mark felt a warmth growing inside him. This was his moment of healing. The years of perseverance and the vulnerability he had allowed himself to feel had brought him to this point. He had climbed not just a mountain, but out of the darkness that had once held him still.

He had found his purpose again, here on the summit of Denali.

Brandon stood beside him, quiet but sharing the moment, as if understanding the depth of what this climb meant to Mark. The view stretched out before them, endless and serene, and for the first time in a long while, Mark felt truly at peace.

They couldn't linger at the summit for long. The altitude was unforgiving, and the cold seeped into their bones. They both knew the descent would be dangerous. It was still part of the climb, and they had to stay alert.

They paused, taking in the view one last time, as if sealing this place, this feeling, in memory.

After a few more minutes, Mark turned to Brandon. "Time to head down."

Brandon smiled, his face set with determination. "Still a lot of mountain left!"

They adjusted their packs, tightened their grip on the ropes, and took the first careful steps of their descent. The summit began to fade behind them, but before they went any further, they both paused, turning back one last time to look at the peak.

In that moment, neither of them spoke, but they didn't need to. Brandon, as he had from the beginning, stood steady beside Mark: silent, loyal, and strong. They both knew that when they reached the bottom, they wouldn't be the same. They had conquered the mountain, but more than that, they had conquered the doubts and fears that had been weighing on them for so long. The climb had tested them, pushed them to their limits, but it had also strengthened their bond in ways words couldn't describe.

As they turned back toward the path ahead, they knew that no matter what challenges still lay ahead, they had climbed not just Denali but toward something bigger, something that would stay with them for the rest of their lives.

With the summit behind them, Mark and Brandon took their first steps back down, forever changed. Each step carried them closer to the world below, but they both knew a part of themselves would stay here, etched into the mountain: a testament to the strength they had found in each other and the purpose they had reclaimed. Denali had tested them, reshaped them, and now they carried its quiet resilience and beauty within, a piece of this summit they would never leave behind.

The Mountain's Voice

Denali stood unchanged, her icy slopes gleaming in the early light. For centuries, she had been a silent guardian of the sky, towering over all who dared to challenge her heights. Many had come. Some had succeeded. Some had not.

Even before the first summit of Denali in 1913, countless climbers had tried to conquer her heights, but the mountain was unforgiving. Crevasses that opened without warning, avalanches that swept away even the most prepared, the deadly grip of altitude sickness: all posed unrelenting threats. Some climbers, in their final moments, had been swallowed by the mountain, lost forever to her glaciers.

Mark and Brandon had witnessed the mountain's dangers firsthand. Early in their ascent, they saw a helicopter circle above, carrying a fallen climber from the escarpment below the ridge to 17,000-Foot Camp. The climber dropped over a hundred feet, and the conditions were too dangerous to attempt a rescue. He froze to death. Later, they learned of another climber who had collapsed and died during the final summit push. Denali did not discriminate. No matter how strong or experienced you were, she could take you at any moment.

When Paul descended to base camp, he passed a group of climbers making their own way up the slope. Days later, one of them would fall into a crevasse, too deep and dangerous to attempt a rescue, while out taking pictures. Another life claimed by Denali's merciless terrain. The mountain had spoken to them in her own way, her icy whispers a constant reminder that this was no ordinary climb. Denali decided who came home.

Yet for all her danger, Denali also granted moments of breathtaking beauty. She revealed sights so pure, so majestic, that those who witnessed them were forever changed. For Mark and Brandon, the summit had been more than just a physical victory. It had been a moment of deep reflection and healing, a gift from the mountain that few would ever understand. Denali had tested them, and in the end, she had allowed them to stand at her peak, if only for a fleeting moment.

Once they were off the mountain, the weight of their achievement settled in. But so did the awareness of the dangers they had left behind. Denali wasn't a mountain you could conquer; she was a force you survived, a challenge you endured. It was the ultimate test of nature and self.

Back in Talkeetna, Mark, Paul, and Brandon visited the cemetery on the outskirts of town that held a memorial of those who had passed away on Denali's slopes. It was a quiet place, unassuming yet filled with the echoes of past climbers. The names engraved on the stones told stories of ambition, of dreams, and of lives lost to the climb. This resting ground carried the memory of those who had come before, climbers who had once stood where they had stood, on Denali's unforgiving slopes.

Standing in the company of the fallen, the trio felt the fragile thread that bound them to these climbers, a silent acknowledgment that their own lives now bore the mountain's mark, a mark that demanded both gratitude and humility.

Paul's thoughts turned briefly to Chad. He had called him not long after the climb, half-expecting to hear the same heaviness that had pressed down on him high on the mountain. Instead, Chad's voice was steadier and lighter. He was finding his rhythm again, piece by piece. Knowing that brought Paul a quiet relief. It was proof that not every story tied to Denali ended in loss.

Mark stood before one of the gravestones, his breath forming small clouds in the crisp Alaskan air. He couldn't help but think of all the fallen climbers who had dreamed of reaching the summit, just as he had.

Brandon knelt beside him, his gloved hand resting gently on the ground. "They're part of the mountain now," he said softly, his voice carrying the weight of what they had been through.

Mark nodded, his gaze still fixed on the gravestone in front of him. He understood now, more than ever, the delicate balance between ambition and respect. Denali was dangerous, but she was also a teacher. She had shown them things about themselves, about their friendship, about life, that they would carry with them forever. But he knew, too, that Denali gave as much as she took, leaving behind pieces of those who had dared her slopes: their fears, their weaknesses, and fragments of themselves scattered across the frozen heights.

"You never know what Denali will bring you," Mark said quietly, "but if you listen to her, she'll grant you sights and memories you'll never forget."

Together, they stood in the quiet stillness of the cemetery, paying their respects to the climbers who had come before them. Denali granted them safe passage and had given them a gift, an experience that would shape the rest of their lives.

Mark knew that part of him would always remain on that mountain, where the line between beauty and danger was so thin, where the echoes of those who had come before whispered in the wind. And as they turned to leave, they knew that no matter where life led them next, Denali would always be with them.

They walked back toward town, each lost in their own thoughts. The air was cold, the sky washed in soft gray, the kind of day that made the world feel both fragile and infinite.

As they got closer to town, Brandon nudged Mark with his elbow, a small grin tugging at the corner of his mouth.

"So," he said, "what's next?"

For a moment, Mark did not answer. He stared toward the distant silhouette of Denali, the giant now half-hidden behind the clouds. The mountain no longer felt like a challenge he had survived. It felt like a door he had passed through.

He exhaled slowly, and even that breath sounded different. It carried thought. The breath of a man who had reclaimed something he thought gone forever.

"Let's go paddle the Stikine River," Mark said.

Brandon and Paul smiled, the kind of smile that carried both surprise and certainty, because in that answer they heard the old Mark again. The one who chased horizons. The one who believed in the next thing.

As they continued down the road, Denali stayed in sight, but its true presence was carried within them, shaping not just where they had been, but where they were going next.

Acknowledgments

This book was born on the slopes of Denali, but it was shaped by the people who clipped into the rope beside me and reminded me that no climb is ever truly solo.

To Mark Schattenberg and Brandon Gabehart: your enduring friendship, inspiration, and humor, on and off the mountain, are the heartbeat of this story. Mark, your strength in the face of pain and uncertainty is the soul of this book. Brandon, your quiet steadiness and loyalty were the rope that held us together, no matter the altitude.

To my parents: thank you for your steadfast support, encouragement, and belief in this journey from the very beginning.

To my wife, whose love, patience, and thoughtful feedback helped guide this book from just an idea to the final page, thank you for being my partner in everything.

Special thanks to Erika Pabst, Mary Delaney, Greetje van Hengel, Natalie Leistikow, Vlad Stefanovici, and Caroline Morris for reading the drafts and offering thoughtful, honest feedback. Your insights helped me see the story with fresh eyes and made the final version stronger, deeper, and truer. I am grateful for your generosity and care.

To everyone who shared in the journey, no matter how big or small, your presence mattered. Whether you offered a word of encouragement, shared in a warm meal, or simply stood witness to the unfolding of this story, I am deeply grateful.

And to Denali: thank you for the lessons etched in ice and silence. You reminded us that not every summit is reached the same way, and that presence, whether on the ridge or from below, can be just as powerful. In your staggering prominence and quiet power, you offered something beyond achievement, something timeless. You held our stories without judgment, and in doing so, gave them room to breathe.

And to those who understand that strength takes many forms: thank you. This book is for anyone who's ever supported from the base, stepped aside so others could reach the summit, or found purpose in the quiet work that makes every summit possible.

About the Author

Paul Schattenberg is an aerospace engineer whose work has reached the moon, yet his gaze often turns back to Earth's wild places. With expertise spanning antenna design and satellite communications, he has spent years building the systems that connect us to space. But it was a mountain that led him to write. Denali: A Journey of Friendship and Perseverance is his first narrative nonfiction work, born from the climb he shared with his brother and a close friend, and from the quiet courage that shaped their story.

First photo post-climb.

Beyond engineering and writing, Paul is a lifelong explorer drawn to both high adventure and subtle wonder. He photographs the stars, flies airplanes, sails open water, dives beneath the waves, and wanders the world chasing moments that make him feel small in the best way. He lives with his wife, Anita, and their beagle, Daisy, and is already sketching the contours of his next escape, one that may become another story worth telling.